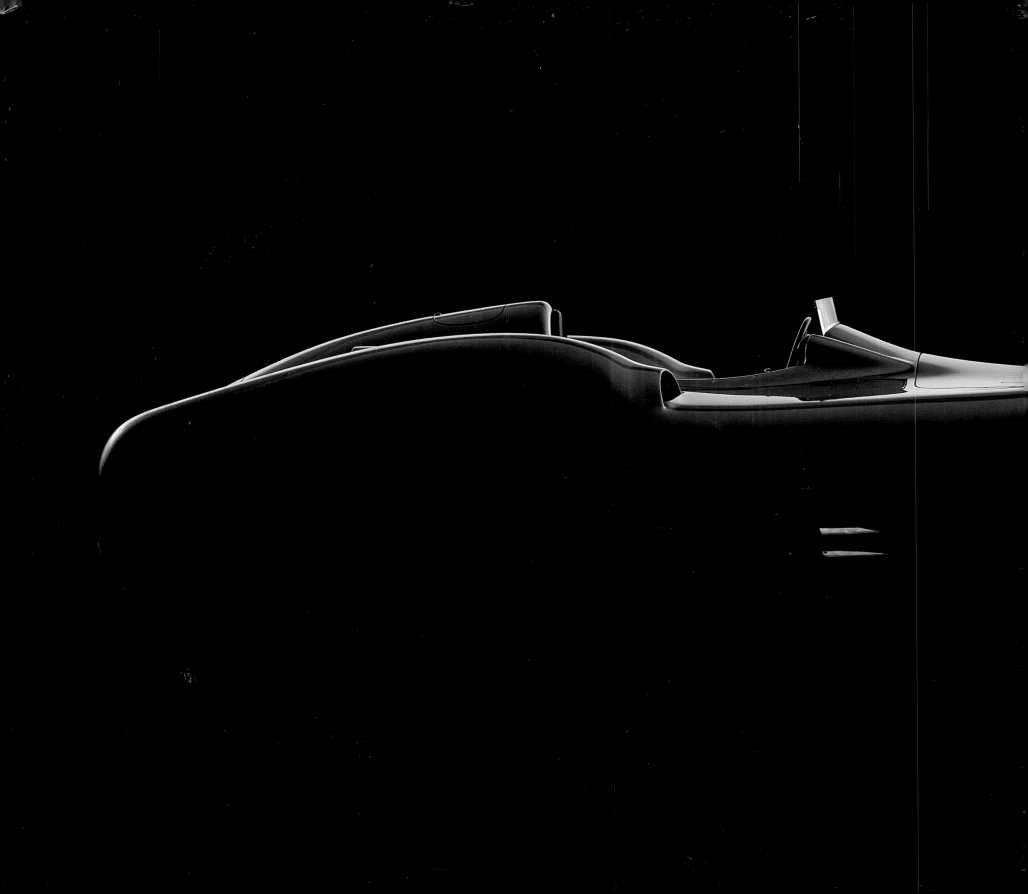

Art of the
Formula 1
Race Car

Stuart Codling with commentary by Gordon Murray

PHOTOGRAPHY BY JAMES MANN

motorbooks

In fond memory of Tom Wheatcroft.

First published in 2010 by Motorbooks, an imprint of MBI Publishing Company, 400 First Avenue North, Suite 300, Minneapolis, MN 55401 USA.

Motorbooks titles are also available at discounts in bulk quantity for industrial or sales-promotional use. For details write to Special Sales Manager at MBI Publishing Company, 400 First Avenue North, Suite 300, Minneapolis, MN 55401 USA.

To find out more about our books, visit us online at www.motorbooks.com.

ISBN-13: 978-0-7603-3731-8

Library of Congress Cataloging-in-Publication Data

Codling, Stuart, 1972-
  Art of the Formula 1 race car / text by Stuart Codling ; photography by James Mann; commentary by Gordon Murray.
    p. cm.
  Includes bibliographical references and index.
  ISBN 978-0-7603-3731-8 (hb w/jkt)
  1. Formula One automobiles. 2. Formula One automobiles—Pictorial works. 3. Grand Prix racing. I. Mann, James, 1963- II. Title.
III. Title: Art of the Formula One race car.
  TL236.C53 2010
  629.228022'2—dc22
                        2009028568

Editor: Jeffrey Zuehlke
Design Manager: Brenda Canales
Designed by: Simon Larkin and Cindy Samargia Laun
Layout by: Cindy Samargia Laun
Cover designed by: Simon Larkin

Printed in China

On the cover:
The McLaren MP4-23 of 2008 Formula 1 World Champion Lewis Hamilton.

On the frontis:
Alfa Romeo 158.

On the title pages:
Mercedes-Benz W196 streamliner.

On the endpapers:
Front: Alfa-Romeo 158; back: Ferrari 312T3.

Contents

Foreword

BY PETER WINDSOR

CAN A FORMULA 1 CAR BE CONSIDERED ART? (And what is "art," anyway?) There is, of course, an art to driving one: The classic manipulative driver's ability to perfectly manage the car's dynamic weight takes him beyond the physical movements of brake, steering, and throttle: His perfection marks the moment when "science" becomes "art"—when human beings step from the merely possible to an altogether different world. Some call it "the zone." Watch a Jim Clark or a Stirling Moss or a Lewis Hamilton in the wet, or on almost-flat fast corners, or on street circuits with no margin for error, and you will certainly be moved to call what they do "art."

Formula 1 cars, however, aren't designed to inspire euphoric essays about aesthetic qualities. If they happen to look pretty then surely that is serendipity. Their beauty, if you can call it that, is of form following function, with the function in question being the simple need for a driver to be transported as quickly and efficiently as possible over a set physical distance. A fast and innovative car is axiomatically beautiful, regardless of its flaws. Indeed, some of the "least-beautiful" F1 cars were in situ kind to the eye because of their function. The 1968 Matra MS10, for instance, looks harsh in a museum alongside a 1961 shark-nosed Ferrari 156. Yet in the wet at the Nürburgring or at Zandvoort, Jackie Stewart–managed, the MS10 was undeniably a thing of stark beauty.

For Enzo Ferrari, Formula 1 was always about the cars; the drivers were of secondary importance (and were replaceable!). This is a reminder that the hallmark of the engineers who build the greatest F1 cars is a restless creative genius.

At Lotus, Colin Chapman epitomized the craftsman-genius. For a while, he made F1 what it was. At Clermont-Ferrand in 1972, I asked Peter Warr, the Lotus team manager, how much life there was yet in the Lotus 72, given that it was entering its third season.

"Well, you never know with Colin," he said. "Look at the oil tank/wing mounting. One day Colin was just looking at the back of the car when suddenly he said, 'Why don't we make the wing mounting serve a dual purpose?' We all looked puzzled, and then a few minutes later he produced a sketch. This sort of thing can go on and on."

Here's to the artists, then—to the men who turned their function into beauty; to the men who captured their images; to the men who drove them and sometimes, when you least expected it, touched the sky with their God-given perfection; and, ultimately, here's to the cars themselves. Mineral they may be; soul-less they are not.

—Peter Windsor, Spring 2009

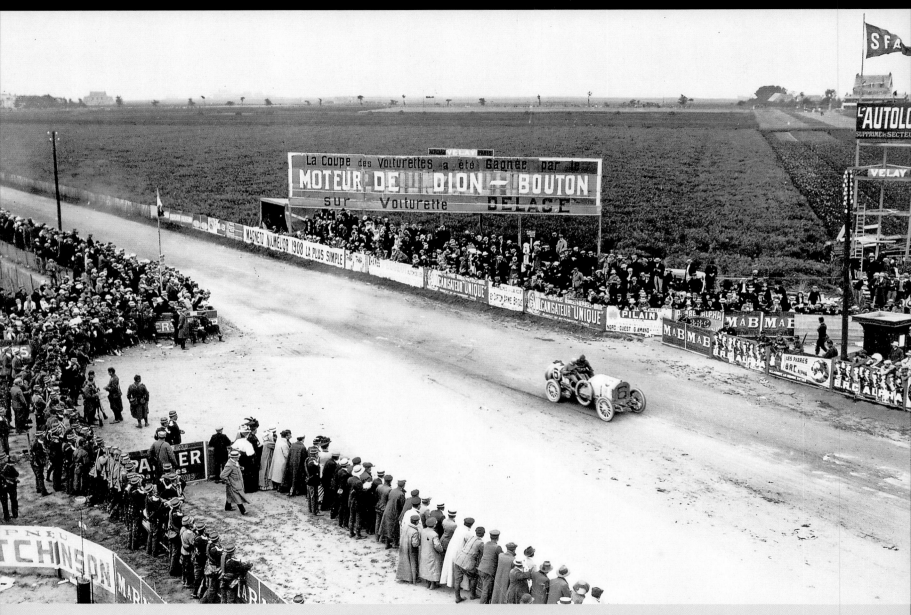

Before the Formula 1 World Championship began in 1950, Grands Prix were organized by local promoters and held on public roads. They were often tests of endurance rather than speed. This is the 1908 French Grand Prix at Dieppe, a gruelling 770km slog along roads that had been badly cut up by the voiturette race the day before. Victor Hémery, seen here, finished second in a Benz 120 hp. Daimler Classic

WHEN YOU WALK INTO THE SUBTERRANEAN ECO-DOME THAT IS the Renault F1 team's Computational Fluid Dynamics Facility, where row upon row of hidden servers crunch unthinkably huge numbers in the name of optimized aerodynamic performance, almost the first thing you see is a replica of the 1898 Voiturette 1CV. This, the very first Renault and a successful racer in its own right, sits facing the centerpiece of the room: a modern Renault F1 car.

To see this is to be reminded that for as long as there have been motorcars, man has sought to race them.

Around the turn of the twentieth century, organized motor races began in Europe, and the first *Grande Epreuve* was held at Le Mans, in France, in 1906. The cars were slow and primitive, driven by aristocrats and nouveau riche industrialists. But time moves on. For the first half of the century, motor racing existed like a deranged experiment in engineering Darwinism: The cars grew from everyday vehicles into specialist racers in a torrent of innovations, barely regulated and lacking anything so cohesive as a championship.

It was only in the reformative years following World War II, when a hardy group of individuals dusted off the prewar Grand Prix cars and began racing again, that the top echelon of motor racing was formalized as Formula 1. It gained a rule book—after a fashion—and, in 1950, a championship for drivers. A constructors' championship followed in 1958.

The early years were difficult. The Alfa Romeos that won the championship in 1950 and 1951 were pre-war dinosaurs, technologically almost irrelevant. Following Alfa's withdrawal in 1951 there just weren't enough F1 cars in circulation to make up the numbers. The sport underwent a crisis of the soul: What was Formula 1 supposed to be? The answer, after allowing in Formula 2 cars for 1952 and 1953, was to rewrite the rules to entice more manufacturers to participate. This evolution of the rule book—alternately seeking to allure as entries dwindle, and to constrain when development gets out of hand—has been a continuous undercurrent of the sport's often self-destructive internal politics ever since.

As Formula 1 gained prominence in the 1950s, the public became more interested. What had been a traveling circus, arriving irregularly and with an ever-changing cast of characters, acquired more fixed points of reference. Of course, people had always been entranced by the noise and spectacle, thronging by the roadside from the earliest days to watch the enormous machines roar past, piloted by daring, enigmatic, otherworldy, untouchable heroes. Now the championship gave form and structure to their passion, put names to faces, provided an ongoing narrative. A specialist press grew up to feed spectators' hunger for knowledge.

The relationship between the press and the participants has always been a fractious one, separated by the simple acts of doing and writing: It is an obvious but largely insurmountable barrier.

And yet it was the specialist press that provided a lifeline to this new constituency of motorsports fans. F1 did not have blanket TV coverage, nor did it (until the 1960s) have much in the way of commercial backing. For the car companies it was a loss leader, of sorts, a means of advertising; for the British privateers—the *garagistes* that Enzo Ferrari curled his lip at—it was a means of selling chassis; and for the drivers it was ceasing to become a way of spending one's inheritance—it was now, through starting money and prizes, a means of earning a living. And all the while, the next generation of gifted engineers—including a young man named Gordon Murray, growing up in South Africa—scoured the motoring magazines, devouring the technical analyses and schematic drawings of Denis Jenkinson, John Bolster, David Phipps, and James Allington.

For all that the drivers—brave, hard-bitten, often effortlessly cool—are the front men of Formula 1, it is the cars that fascinate. Perhaps, to an extent, Enzo Ferrari was right in viewing the cars—*his* cars—as the stars, and the drivers as mere employees, as easily interchangeable as the parts of a lawnmower. The engineers who designed and built those cars were seldom venerated by the public to the same extent as a champion driver, and yet it was their inspiration and labor (right up until the 1970s, F1 designers worked alone or in a very small group) that furnished the entire spectacle.

Unlike today, the great engineers of F1's earlier age had neither the time nor the resources to engage in endless research. Wind tunnels, such as they were, accepted only quarter-scale models (at best) and had no rolling road, so their results were only of marginal accuracy—especially if the model was an agglomeration of balsawood, Plasticine, and sticky tape. The likes of Colin Chapman were restless, driven, energetic, questing; always

Mercedes raised the level of engineering and preparation when it returned to F1 in 1954. Stirling Moss (left) and runner-up Juan Manuel Fangio finished one-two in the 1955 British Grand Prix at Aintree. Daimler Classic

Bernie Ecclestone (right) with Carlos Reutemann (center) and Gordon Murray at the 1975 Argentine GP. After trying his luck as a driver in the 1950s, Ecclestone emerged as a driver manager in the 1960s before buying the Brabham team. He would go on to revolutionize F1's commercial arrangements. LAT Photographic

Colin Chapman inspects the work of one of his rivals at the 1966 French Grand Prix at Reims. Top engineers were as intensely competitive as the drivers. LAT Photographic

looking for the next big idea, making one component do two or more jobs. Lighter, leaner, faster was the mantra. And they were every bit as competitive with each other as the drivers were: When Murray unveiled the extraordinary Brabham BT46 "fan car" at the 1978 Swedish GP, Chapman's very public outrage at this blatant circumvention of the rules masked a burning jealousy that he, Chapman, hadn't thought of it first.

In an interview with *F1 Racing* magazine, the former Lotus designer Martin Ogilvie described Chapman's manic, obsessive approach: "The worst time to deal with Colin was when he got enthused about something. We had to deliver in no time at all and work all hours. His mantra was to always 'double it' or 'half it.' He'd waltz into the office and say, 'Right, next year I want double the downforce.'

"There was one occasion when Colin said to me, 'I want you to design the rear anti-roll bar to be twice as stiff. And I mean *twice as stiff*.' He was quite explicit. So I built this huge, heavy, anti-roll bar which was totally hopeless, of course. And he was aghast and told me: 'Ah, Martin, you must always design what I mean, not what I say. I was just making the point for emphasis.'"

Besides spurring his staff on to attempt the barely possible, Chapman had a genius for assessing a design at a glance—"if it looks right, then it is right," as the old saying goes—on his regular rounds of the design office. "Without missing a beat," recalled Ogilvie, "he'd point to something and say, 'Not like that.' And you'd think, 'Bloody hell, he's right!' He'd spot something that he didn't like, that wasn't elegant or that he knew wasn't going to work. Then he'd just breeze out again."

Money, in the form of sponsorship, began rushing in to Formula 1 in the 1960s. Barring the oil crises of the early 1970s and a brief blip at the beginning of the 1990s, it has been a veritable Niagara. The fashionable view is that the majority of this money vanishes into the pocket (via a network of shell companies and offshore bank accounts) of Bernard Charles Ecclestone, the former motorcycle dealer who turned the sport into a properly commercial entity. Ecclestone takes his cut, but there has been plenty to go around—enough to make multimillionaires of many team bosses, senior engineers, and drivers, and to fund massive investment in engineering staff and technology. In the 1970s, the average race staff of an F1 team could be transported, at a pinch, in a pair of Ford Cortinas. Thirty years later, the average staff of a team is some way north of 500 people.

The days when a senior engineer could be quite so hands-on are long gone. I once asked Patrick Head, the director of engineering at Williams, about how the design process had evolved.

"It's true that in the 1970s, '80s, and even the early '90s I could walk down a line of drawing boards and look over somebody's shoulder," he said. "I could be in on Sundays, or in the evening, and have a look at their work. I could leave notes on their desk. I could direct the design. If I saw something that I could think of a way of doing better, I could put something up on my drawing board, work out the idea, then show it to them. Now, with it all on CAD screens, when they go home the screen goes blank. You can set up systems to access it, but it's not necessarily as visible. That's why you have to set up an approach appropriate to the tools we have at the moment."

When Gordon Murray quit F1 at the end of the 1980s, it was because he felt that the rules had become so restrictive that there was no room to innovate: Design had become procedural, a numbing grind of fettling and optimizing an existing product.

There were no great leaps in performance to be found. The scientists had invaded the wind tunnel; aerodynamic research had progressed beyond instinct into a realm of fixed reference points and "repeatability." The models were half-size or built to scale, assembled with pinpoint precision, every detail already ratified by computer. To an instinctive and intuitive engineer like Murray, this was anathema.

Technology may have drowned out the brilliance of the individualists, but the momentum has been unstoppable: Until just before the last global economic upset, no self-respecting F1 team could call itself competitive unless it had not one but two wind tunnels, at least one of which was full-scale, and both running 24 hours a day. That is what Head meant when he talked about developing an approach to suit the tools of the moment.

However, throughout the decades, one thing has not changed: the passion. A senior F1 designer recently told me that one of the most beautiful pieces of engineering he'd ever seen, in terms of attention to detail and absence of compromise, was the steering mechanism of the Tyrrell six-wheeler. By most contemporary yardsticks, that car was not a success, and yet its sheer ambition beggars parallel; it was designed and constructed in secret, not just by Tyrrell engineers but with collaboration from the likes of Goodyear, which found tires to suit the front wheels, and Ferodo, which made the diminutive brake pads. It is not an especially pretty car in either specification, but it has a distinctive beauty—an artfulness, if you like—that demands admiration.

The history of Formula 1 is an epic narrative, replete with tragedies and triumphs; and the fabric of this tapestry is not the individual heroism of the people who drive the cars, but the dozens of often-unheralded individuals hunched over drawing boards and CAD screens, each adhering to the mantra of the great engineers: nothing is unimproveable, only unimproved.

An example of F1's spectacular growth: When Bruce McLaren formed his eponymous team in 1963, the company's first "headquarters" was a shed with a dirt floor. In 2004, The McLaren Group opened the multi-million dollar McLaren Technology Centre, which covers 50 hectares in Woking, Surrey. www.mclaren.com

Aerodynamic testing has progressed from informed guesswork (often verified by attaching wool tufts to the cars) to full-scale experimentation in dedicated multi-million dollar wind tunnel facilities like the one shown here at the McLaren Technology Centre. www.mclaren.com

Alfa Romeo 158/159

SUCH A THING WOULD NEVER HAPPEN in modern Formula 1: When Giuseppe Farina took the checkered flag at Silverstone on May 13, 1950, on his way to becoming the first Formula 1 World Champion, he did so in a car that had been designed thirteen years earlier. That car, newly restored and one of only two remaining in the world, is pictured here.

In late 1937, Enzo Ferrari, Alfa Romeo's racing manager, was locked in a political battle with the Spanish engineer Wilfredo Ricart. To all intents and purposes, Ferrari had been sidelined when Alfa bought 80 percent of his team and installed Ricart over his head. Alfa's racing activities were chaotic: Ricart, working from the Alfa factory in Portello, attempted to build a Grand Prix car that could take on the all-conquering Mercedes and Auto Union Machine; Ferrari, realizing that it would be hopeless to try to compete against the free-spending Germans, commissioned Gioacchino Colombo to build a smaller, lighter car for the voiturette (French for "little car") class. The projects proceeded independently of one another, with Ferrari supervising his project in his own workshops in Modena until his rancorous relationship with Ricart became intolerable, after which Alfa and Ferrari parted ways.

Colombo's neat voiturette was called the 158, deriving its name from its engine's capacity (1.5 liters) and number of cylinders (eight). With a Roots supercharger plumbed in, the little straight eight was good for almost 200 horsepower, transmitting that

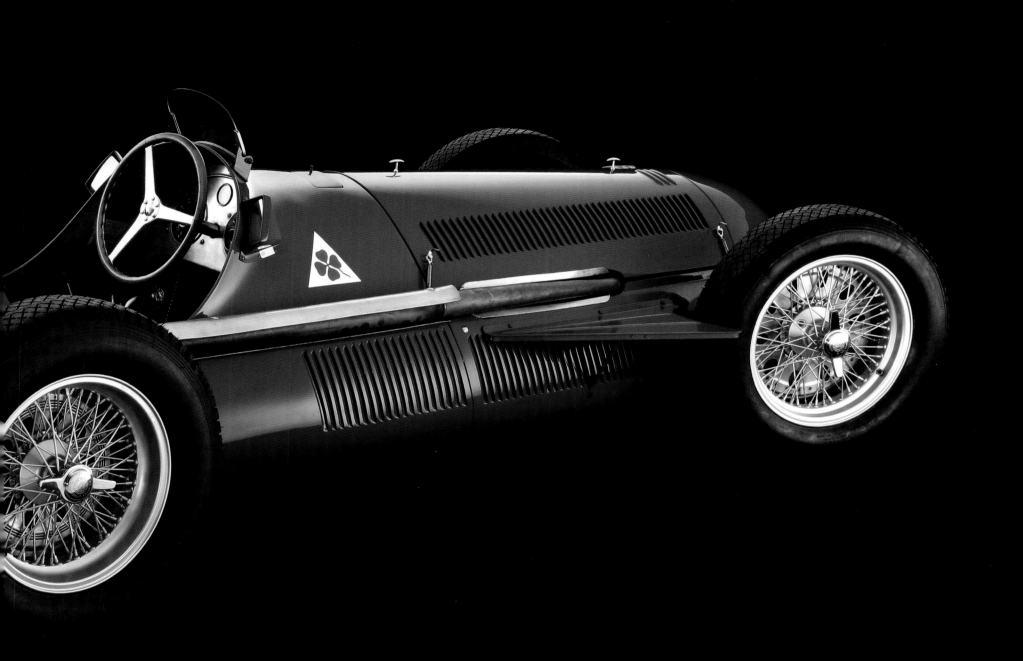

power to the road via a four-speed transaxle. The chassis was agricultural but typical of the time: leaf springs all round, with a swing axle at the rear and trailing arms up front—and, of course, drum brakes.

After the outbreak of World War II, the 158s were concealed in a small village near Gorgonzola, just east of Milan, where they miraculously escaped being melted down for munitions. By 1950, Alfa Romeo was back in action on the international racing scene and a regular winner in the Grands Prix that permitted voiturettes.

The 1950 Formula 1 season, now a world championship, permitted two engine types: 1.5-liter supercharged and 4.5-liter naturally aspirated. For the opening GP of the year, at Silverstone in Britain, Alfa Romeo finished one-two-three. Giuseppe Farina won, followed by Luigi Fagioli and Reg Parnell. The only disappointment for Alfa was that Juan Manuel Fangio was forced to retire his 158. Apart from its historical significance, the 1950 British GP wasn't a notable race; the nearest other finishers were two laps down.

The 158 was a delicate and not especially sure-handling device, but by now its engine had been modified to produce over 250 horsepower, which gave it a decisive speed advantage over the superannuated old clunkers that were predominantly arranged against it. Alfa won six of the seven world championship rounds (and skipped the Indy 500, which counted to the championship even though most Europeans did not attend) and five non-championship races in 1950; the only credible opposition came from Scuderia Ferrari. Enzo had a score to settle, and in the final race of the season Alberto Ascari finished second in the new 4.5-liter V-12 Ferrari 375.

Alfa could no longer take it easy. By the end of 1950, it had produced four new chassis, designated 159, with de Dion tube rear suspension in place of the swing-axle setup. An additional supercharger brought the straight eight's output to around 400 horsepower. The dreadful fuel consumption concomitant with this power boost required Alfa to fit a larger tank.

1950 British Grand Prix. Silverstone, Great Britain. Guiseppe Farina leads an Alfa Romeo romp to begin the Formula 1 era. LAT Photographic

Like the cars they drove, the 1950 Alfa Romeo team's drivers were of decidedly prewar vintage: (L-R) Future five-time World Champion Juan Manuel Fangio, 1950 World Champion Giuseppe Farina, Felice Bonetto, and Emmanuel de Graffenried. LAT Photographic

In the first race of 1951, the Swiss GP at Bremgarten, Fangio shot off into the lead, with his teammates—and Ferrari's Piero Taruffi—in pursuit. Farina attempted to seize the initiative with a cunning economy run, soft-pedaling his 159 in the hope that he could get around without pitting. While he tussled with Taruffi, Fangio stopped for more fuel and was quick enough to catch and pass them both, winning by almost a minute.

Farina won the Belgian GP from Ferrari's Alberto Ascari by nearly three minutes after Fangio got stuck in the pits with a jammed wheel. But this winning margin didn't accurately reflect the narrowing performance gap between the two marques: Next time out, at Reims, Ascari blasted into the lead at the start, only to retire early with gearbox problems. At Silverstone, the fifth round, José Froilán González put a 375 on pole and only briefly lost the lead on his way to outright victory. Apart from the Indy 500, which no European marques attended, this was the first world championship race to have been won by a car other than an Alfa Romeo.

In one final push for victory, Alfa beefed up its chassis rails and cranked up the superchargers to produce the 420-horsepower 159M (for "Maggiorata"—literally "increased"). All but one of the cars expired at Monza, leaving Fangio to face the final Grand Prix of the year with only a two-point advantage over Ascari. At Pedralbes it was Ferrari's turn to err: Fearful that the half shafts of his cars would be stressed to breaking point by the street circuit's cobbles, he put 16-inch wheels on instead of the regular 17-inchers. Ascari put his car on pole, but in the race his tires shredded and he trailed home in fourth, while Fangio won—despite stopping twice for fuel.

It was to be the first of five drivers' titles for Fangio, but the end of the Grand Prix road for Alfa Romeo. Only Ferrari had made cars to the 4.5-liter formula, and with no other takers, the Fédération Internationale de l'Automobile (FIA) was

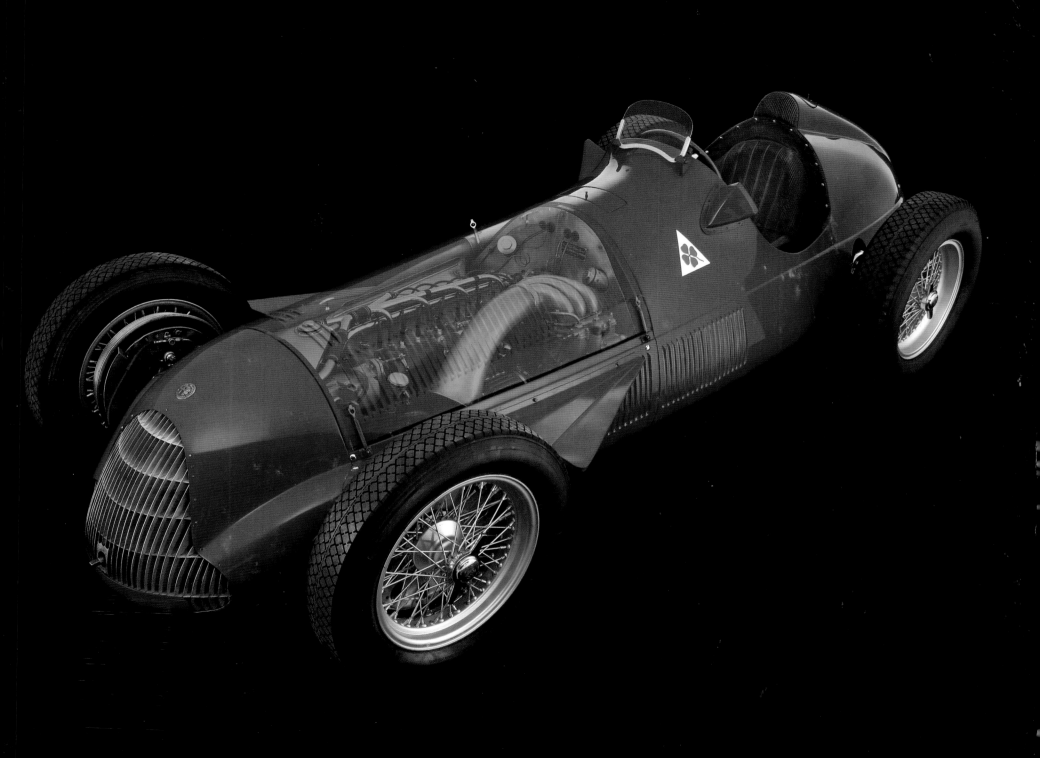

forced to announce a 2.5-liter formula to come into effect in 1954. The prewar voiturettes were exhausted and obsolete, and the 159s had been developed far beyond a point that was sensible.

Alfa Romeo, faced with a choice between building a new car that would only have a two-season lifespan or concentrating on sports car racing, declared the 159s finished and withdrew from F1. Other manufacturers, such as Lago-Talbot, did likewise. At the time, this must have seemed a sensible option: F1 was in flux and poorly supported, whereas the sports car scene was thriving in a Europe still bearing the social and economic scars of World War II.

Not for the first or last time, Enzo Ferrari was poised to capitalize on the change, having a Formula 2 car ready when the FIA decided that to keep numbers up it would allow F2 cars into the world championship in 1952 and 1953. His name would forever be associated with F1; whereas Alfa Romeo, barring a brief and largely unsuccessful comeback in the late 1970s, resides chiefly in the dusty outer reaches of the sport's history.

This is one of my favorite cars from the era. I grew up surrounded by books full of this kind of thing. At this time, the main area of development was in the powertrain—the engines and transmission were where they made huge strides. The chassis were fairly crude, and they stayed that way until Mercedes arrived with a properly stress-tested space frame.

Gordon Murray

Alfa Romeo 158/159

First championship GP
Great Britain (Silverstone), 1950

Last championship GP
Spain (Pedralbes), 1956

Wins/championship races entered
10/13

Wins

Great Britain (Silverstone)	1950	Farina
Monaco (Monte Carlo)	1950	Fangio
Switzerland (Bremgarten)	1950	Farina
Belgium (Spa-Francorchamps)	1950	Fangio
France (Reims-Gueux)	1950	Fangio
Italy (Monza)	1950	Farina
Switzerland (Bremgarten)	1951	Fangio
Belgium (Spa-Francorchamps)	1951	Farina
France (Reims-Gueux)	1951	Fangio *
Spain (Pedralbes)	1951	Fangio

Engine
1,479-cc Alfa-Romeo straight eight, supercharged, 200–420 horsepower (est.)

* Fangio took over Fagioli's car.

2
Maserati 250F

THE EARLY TO MID-1950s WAS AN ERA of sparsely populated Formula 1 grids and but a handful of races a year. But the new 2.5-liter engine rule for 1954 provided the catalyst for rapid change, prompting Maserati, among others, to produce a low-cost car for private customers. Maserati snapped up engineer Gioacchino Colombo from Alfa Romeo and set to work.

Although exalted by many as the quintessential front-engined Formula 1 car, the Maserati 250F has been dismissed by revisionist historians as little more than a dinosaur itself. Certainly its results don't justify the hype: During the Maserati works team's four seasons (1954–1957), the 250F won just eight world championship Grands Prix. But the chassis was a triumph of industrial engineering against the odds: designed, fabricated, and assembled in remarkable quantities with enormous passion by a small number of people. The 250F was on the grid at the first and last Grands Prix of the 2.5-liter era—a remarkable seven-season run. It filled out the grids at a time when Formula 1 was struggling to justify itself. And it provided a means for talented drivers to race cost-effectively at the top level for several years.

How many were built? It's hard to say, for the factory's attitude to bookkeeping was lackadaisical, and chassis and engines were borrowed and swapped to suit the moment. Customer desperate to have a car back from a rebuild? Pop someone else's engine in for now and then sort it out later. . . .

The 250F launched many a career, including that of Stirling Moss. The young privateer racer is shown here on the front row of the grid before the start of the 1954 non-championship Daily Express International Trophy Race at Silverstone. LAT Photographic

A squadron of Maserati 250Fs at rest in the garage at Spa-Francorchamps before the 1958 Belgian Grand Prix. LAT Photographic

The 250F began as a development of Maserati's F2 car, with a 2.5-liter unsupercharged V-6 engine to suit the new regulations. Its chassis was a complex space frame clad with aluminum panels. It had independent suspension at the front and leaf springs at the rear—a conventional layout with a twist, since Maserati had followed Ferrari in locating the de Dion tube ahead of the live axle, in front of the transmission's final drive. Moving this mass forward improved the weight distribution and freed up space for the fuel tank to move forward too. The driver had to sit with his legs apart, straddling the clutch housing, with the brake pedal on the right and the clutch and accelerator on the left.

Interest from Juan Manuel Fangio led Maserati to form a works team in addition to the customer operation (even though he was signed to race for Mercedes when its cars were ready), a move that pushed the already stretched production process beyond breaking point. The first batch of customer cars weren't ready for the first race of the 1954 season, and Maserati had to appease its customers by furnishing a number of F2 chassis with the 2.5-liter engine shoehorned in.

Entering the first race—Fangio's home Grand Prix in Argentina—without much testing rapidly revealed some inherent problems. In combination with grippy new tires, the chassis was too stiff for the suspension to cope with the cornering loads; the engineers had to cut tubes out of the space frame to allow more flex. The engine had a tendency toward oil incontinence, partly through inexact assembly of the pipes, but mostly because the oil tank was mounted by the engine, under the carburetor, where it overheated. All but one blew up during practice; equipped with the last "fresh" engine, Fangio won the race (controversially, after the organizers ignored a protest from Ferrari).

In the gap between the Argentine Grand Prix in January and the Belgian Grand Prix in June, Maserati assuaged its irate customers with a flow of new chassis and worked on the 250F's reliability problems. It

Juan Manuel Fangio at Spa-Francorchamps in Belgium en route to his and the 250F's second consecutive victory to open the 1954 season. Fangio would make it three in a row in France—but he would take that win behind the wheel of a Mercedes-Benz. LAT Photographic

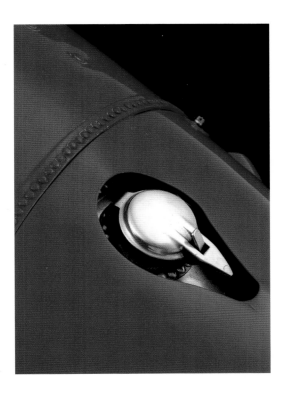

relocated the oil tank to a cooler place—although the integrity of the plumbing was still suspect—and, aided by the absence of the new Lancia and Mercedes, won in Belgium.

One of the customers during the 1954 season was Stirling Moss, who had returned from a trip to the United States to find that his family had ordered a 250F for him with financial backing from Shell-Mex and BP. Having been turned down for a works drive by Mercedes on account of his inexperience, Moss found the sweet-handling 250F an ideal platform to demonstrate his skills. He finished third to Fangio in Belgium and may even have won the Italian GP—humbling Mercedes along the way—but for a split oil tank. The Mercedes works seat was his for 1955.

The 250F photographed here—chassis number 2513—was also a customer car and has a fascinating story of its own: Tony Vandervell, one of the original backers of BRM, bought it in 1954 as a rolling chassis without bodywork or engine for his own Vanwall Formula 1 team to use as reference. They stripped it and weighed, measured, and photographed every component. Vanwall was never able to replicate the 250F's predictable handling, but the team's efforts did produce a car good enough to win the constructors' championship in 1958.

Maserati's engineers churned out developments in a somewhat unstructured way, and many of them yielded little or no benefit. They produced a streamlined variant with enclosed bodywork in 1955, but it tended to set fire to the body panels around the exhaust enclosure; in its only race outing, it expired as Jean Behra crossed the finish line in fourth place at Monza. Ironically enough, the prototype was destroyed in a factory fire. The muddled development process left Maserati unable to capitalize on the withdrawal of Mercedes at the end of 1955. After a confused 1956 season, the manufacturer decided to stop building customer cars and refocused on a three-car factory assault for 1957 led by Fangio.

The 1957 250F T2 was lighter, used thinner-gauge tubing in the space frame, and had bigger brakes and better streamlining. This was the definitive 250F, and Fangio won the last of his five world championships in it, sealing the title with two rounds to go. But a new generation of lighter, faster British cars was emerging that made even the T2 look like a lumbering behemoth.

Learning that fuel additives would be banned for the 1958 season, Maserati embarked on a final frenzy of development, experimenting first with a flat-12 engine, then with a V-12, then finally shelving both—along with a putative new chassis—when the money ran out. Maserati withdrew from Formula 1 at the end of 1957 and went into receivership in April 1958. By then, Moss had won the season-opening Argentine Grand Prix in a Cooper T43—the first Formula 1 victory for a mid-engined chassis, signifying the beginning of the end for the front-engined car.

American investor Temple Buell bought the final batch of 250Fs, including the short-tailed "Piccolo" variant, and carried on racing. At the final race of the 1960 season, the last Grand Prix before the new 1.5-liter formula, Bob Drake brought the 250F's remarkable career to an appropriately plucky conclusion—in the face of more modern mid-engined machinery, he qualified his three-year-old car and finished 13th.

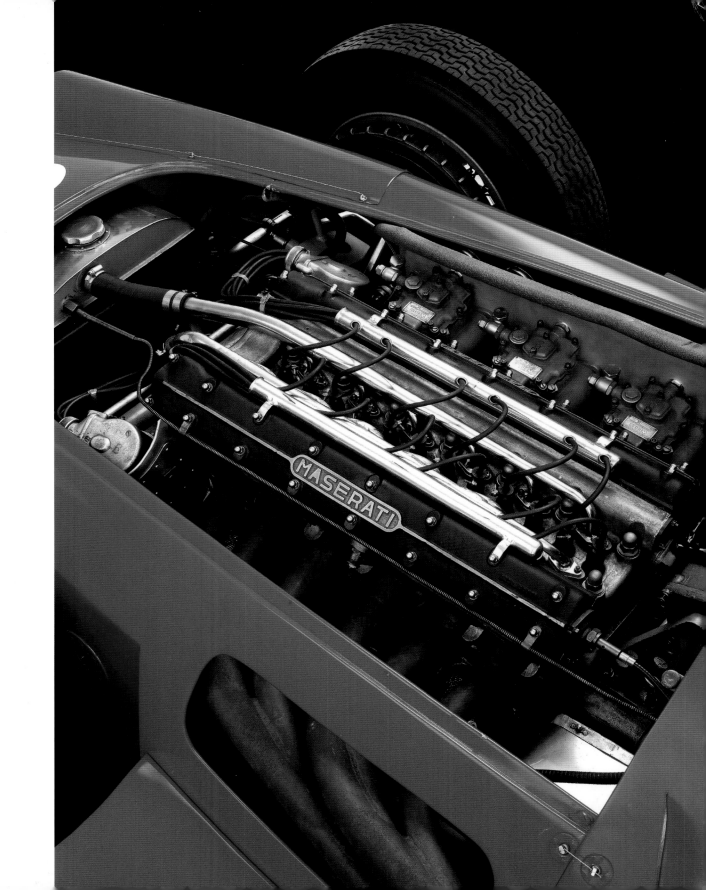

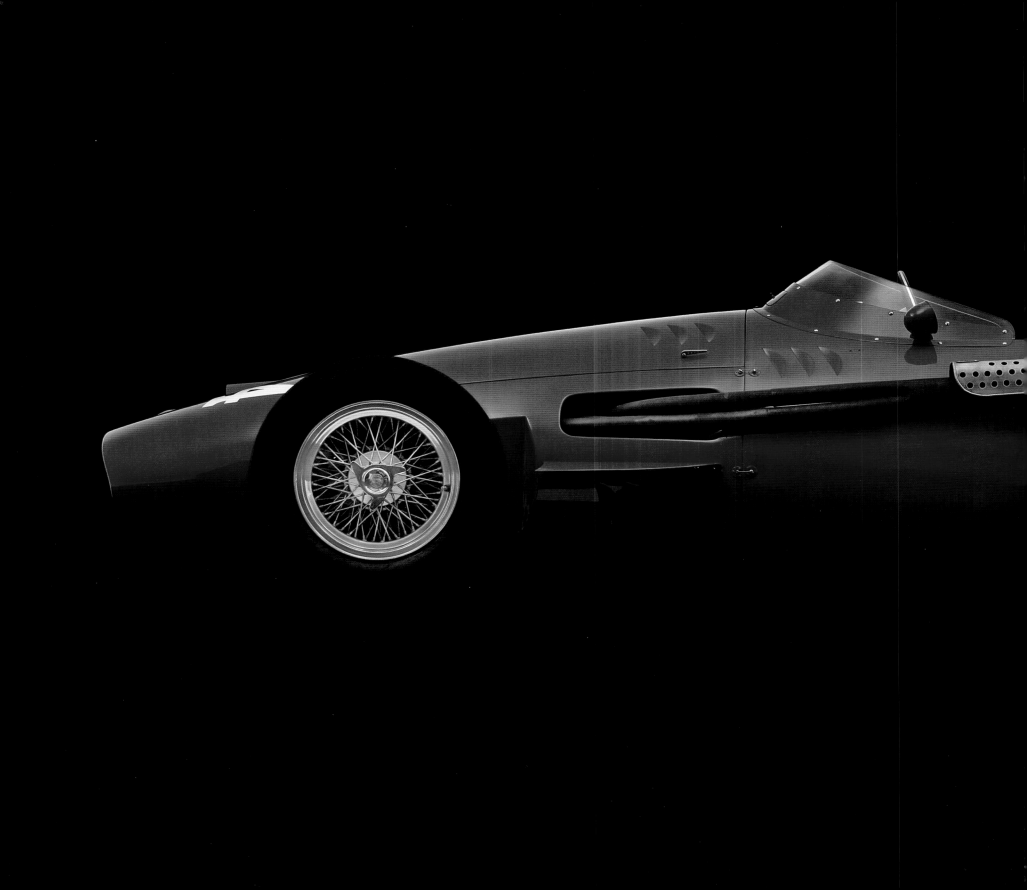

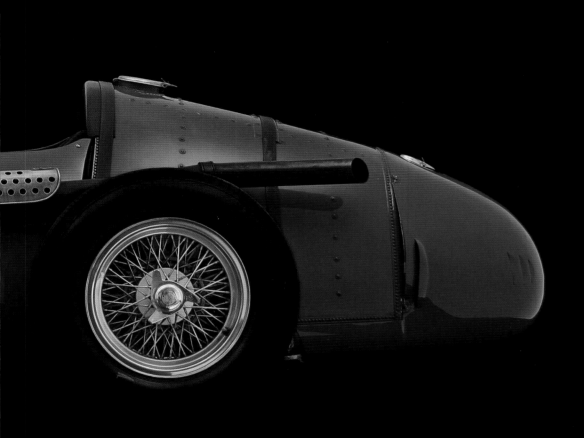

Another classic, and probably one of the better-balanced cars of the time from a driving point of view. It was also one of the first attempts to lower the driveline to benefit the center of gravity. If you compare it with other cars of the time it's substantially lower. In the engineering detail, the forging is really good. It's the welding that lets it down. That was a bit crude. And the basic concept of the chassis, the type of suspension and the torsion and bending—that was way behind the engine design. But it's an elegant, classic look, with simple compound curves and little gills. When I designed the Rocket road car I took my cue from cars like this.

Gordon Murray

Maserati 250F

First championship GP
Argentina (Buenos Aires), 1954

Last championship GP
United States (Riverside), 1960

Wins/championship races entered
8/46

Wins

Argentina (Buenos Aires)	1954	Fangio
Belgium (Spa-Francorchamps)	1954	Fangio
Monaco (Monte Carlo)	1956	Moss
Italy (Monza)	1956	Moss
Argentina (Buenos Aires)	1957	Fangio
Monaco (Monte Carlo)	1957	Fangio
France (Reims)	1957	Fangio
Germany (Nürburgring)	1957	Fangio

Engine
2,494-cc, Maserati straight six, 240 horsepower (est.)
2,491-cc, Maserati V-12, 270 horsepower (est.)

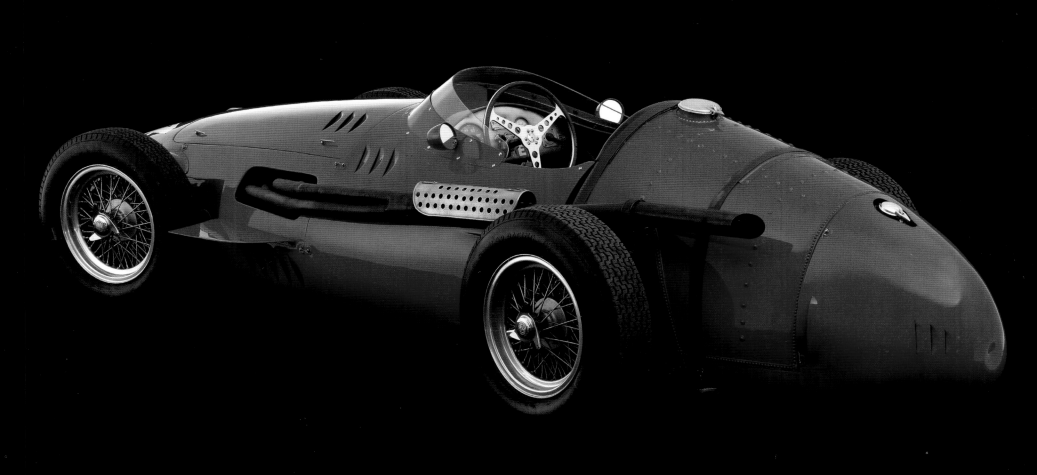

3
Mercedes–Benz W196

MERCEDES-BENZ HAD DOMINATED prewar Grand Prix racing, and in July 1954 the manufacturer exploded back onto the scene with a car that looked like no other. It would prove to be a brief return, for less than 18 months later Mercedes would withdraw from motor racing in the wake of the Le Mans disaster. But the detailed engineering of the W196 and the sheer professionalism of the team's approach revolutionized Formula 1.

In early July, at the French Grand Prix at Reims, after months of feverish anticipation, Mercedes unveiled the W196 and promptly took up where it had left off in 1939. The streamlined bodywork had been designed specifically for tracks where sustained top speeds were crucial to a quick lap time; Mercedes had an open-wheeled variant under development for the rest of the Formula 1 calendar. And the team had a potent driver combination, having lured the mighty Juan Manuel Fangio from Maserati to join German stars Karl Kling and Hans Herrmann.

The Reims course, which was no more complex than a huge triangle formed from flat, open public roads, made a perfect match for the streamliner. During practice, Fangio earned himself 50 bottles of champagne from the organizers for lapping at an average of over 200 kilometers per hour.

Seconds after the starter's flag fell, Fangio and Kling were side-by-side under the Dunlop Bridge and accelerating away, already more than a hundred yards ahead of the field. They finished one-two, staging

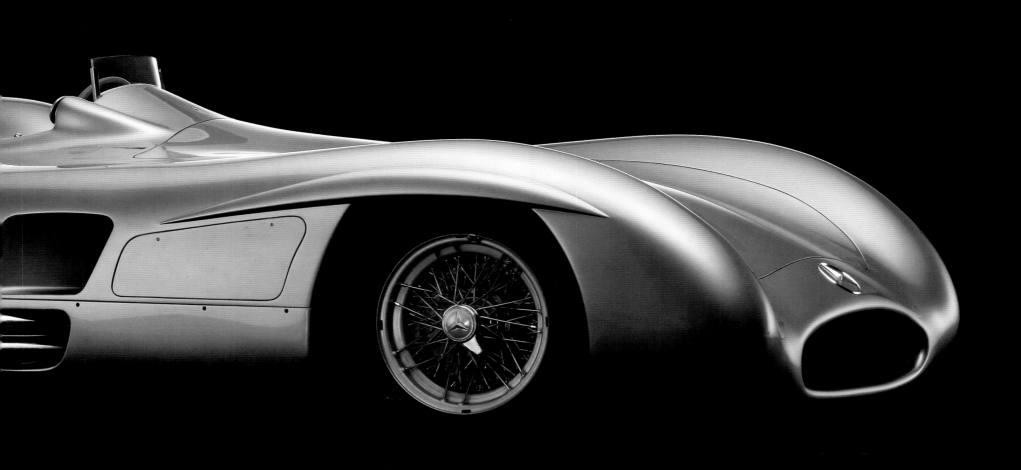

34

a mock duel over the closing laps to entertain the crowd, and crossed the line a lap ahead of the nearest finisher. "One could almost picture Fangio asking Kling what he was going to have for dinner, as the two cars ran side-by-side at about 175 mph," wrote Gregor Grant in *Autosport*.

So furious had been the pace that only six other cars made it to the end. Mercedes-Benz's return to Grand Prix racing seemed to herald the dawn of a depressingly dominant era; for their competitors, the only crumb of hope came from the fact that Herrmann's engine had blown—albeit after setting the fastest lap.

In truth, the W196 was only just ready for competition, even after missing the first three championship races, and its vulnerabilities would become apparent over the following months. In a straight line, it was outrageously fast, but it was unstable under braking, and even under Fangio's finessed superintendence it wouldn't power slide elegantly around corners. It looked hairy during practice at Reims, even more so after the sports cars and Maseratis had deposited oil around the course.

Mercedes advanced the art of Formula 1 engineering in almost every aspect of the W196's design. Using experience derived from the 300SL sports car project, chief designer Rudolf Uhlenhaut created a space frame chassis that was a masterpiece of detailing, each tube stress-tested to achieve the optimal balance of strength and lightness. To overcome the potential weight disadvantage of the bodywork, he turned to the aeronautics industry for inspiration and used magnesium alloy, one of the lightest and most advanced materials of the time, but not one that you'd wish to be enclosed inside during a fire. With a bespoke racing engine—a fuel-injected, desmodromic-valved, straight eight hopped up on all manner of fuel additives and laid on its side in the chassis, 20 degrees from the horizontal in order to give the bodywork a wind-cheating profile—it could out-accelerate any other car on the grid.

Flat out on Monza's lethal banking: Juan Manuel Fangio and Stirling Moss in W196 "streamliners" lead Karl Kling's open-wheeled W196 in the 1955 Italian GP. It was to be Mercedes' last Grand Prix for almost four decades. DaimlerClassic

Stirling Moss took his first Formula 1 victory aboard an open-wheel W196 in the British Grand Prix at Aintree in 1955, much to the delight of the home crowd. DaimlerClassic

To reduce unsprung weight—but at the cost of harder access—Uhlenhaut mounted the brakes inboard, requiring greater cooling: This was what gave the streamliner and its more conventional sister car a distinctive gaping maw. At the front, the huge drums had very fine radial finning within aluminum shrouds to boost the airflow; to accommodate all this in the low-profile bodywork, engine included, was a supreme feat of packaging.

The rear featured a less happy arrangement. Swing-axle suspension—where the rear wheels are attached by two pivoting half axles—had the advantage of independent springing, but under hard cornering, it suffered massive camber change. Even at the time, it was viewed as unsuitable for racing applications, and some observers believed that the directive had originated from the marketing department—Mercedes' new range of production cars were similarly suspended. Even with the pivot point in the center, under the differential, it was not ideal, and many believed that the car's handling was flattered by Fangio's skill. Kling and Herrmann could be quick over a single lap but usually struggled for consistency over a race distance.

The fit and finish of the W196 was superior to any other car on the grid, as was the presentation and organizational efficiency of the Mercedes team. After an early hiccup—the open-wheeler wasn't ready in time for the next GP at Silverstone, and Fangio kept biffing the corner markers because he couldn't see the streamliner's extremities—the team won three more Grands Prix that season, one with the streamliner at Monza (it also won a non-championship race at Avus).

The streamliner model had a last hurrah in 1955 at Monza, held on an extended version of the road circuit that incorporated the newly built banked section. After Fangio tested a streamliner back-to-back with the open-wheeler and found it two seconds a lap quicker, Mercedes had the other remaining one shipped in and hastily prepped for Stirling Moss. Fangio won, clinching his third drivers' title, but Mercedes had already decided to withdraw from motorsports after this final round of the season.

It would be almost four decades before the three-pointed star graced a Formula 1 car again.

The aesthetics are fantastic. From an engineering point of view, you've got all three things working together now: the chassis, with a multi-tubular space frame; the engine, which was very advanced; and the third element is the aerodynamic sophistication. Before, there had been attempts to streamline the cars, but they never went that far—they were all generically the same sort of shape, with the rear-mounted cockpit, long nose, and rounded or pointy tail. But this shape is clearly the product of lots of thought. The thing that amazed me about this era of Mercedes-Benz was the swing-axle suspension. Mind you, they were all single-person cars—just one engineer responsible for the whole layout—so it may just have been their 'thing.' But it does let it down—even though it had a low pivot center, it was still a swing axle.

Gordon Murray

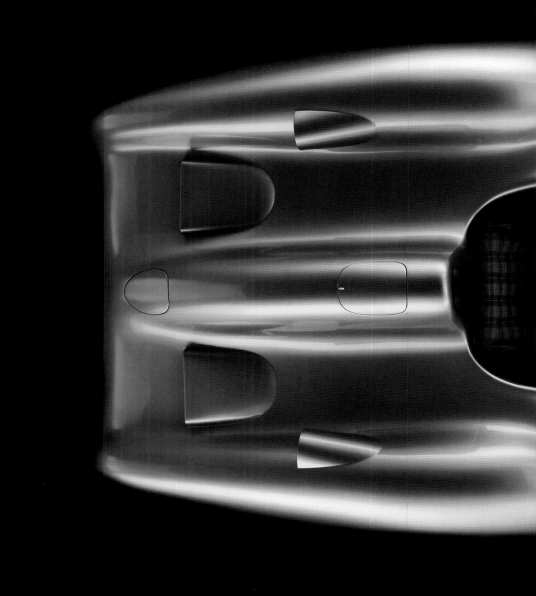

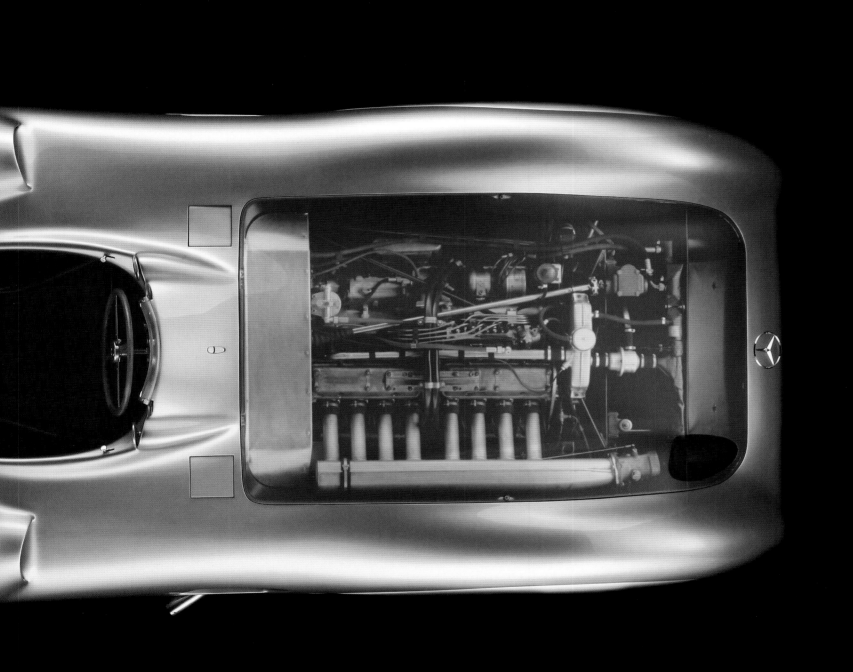

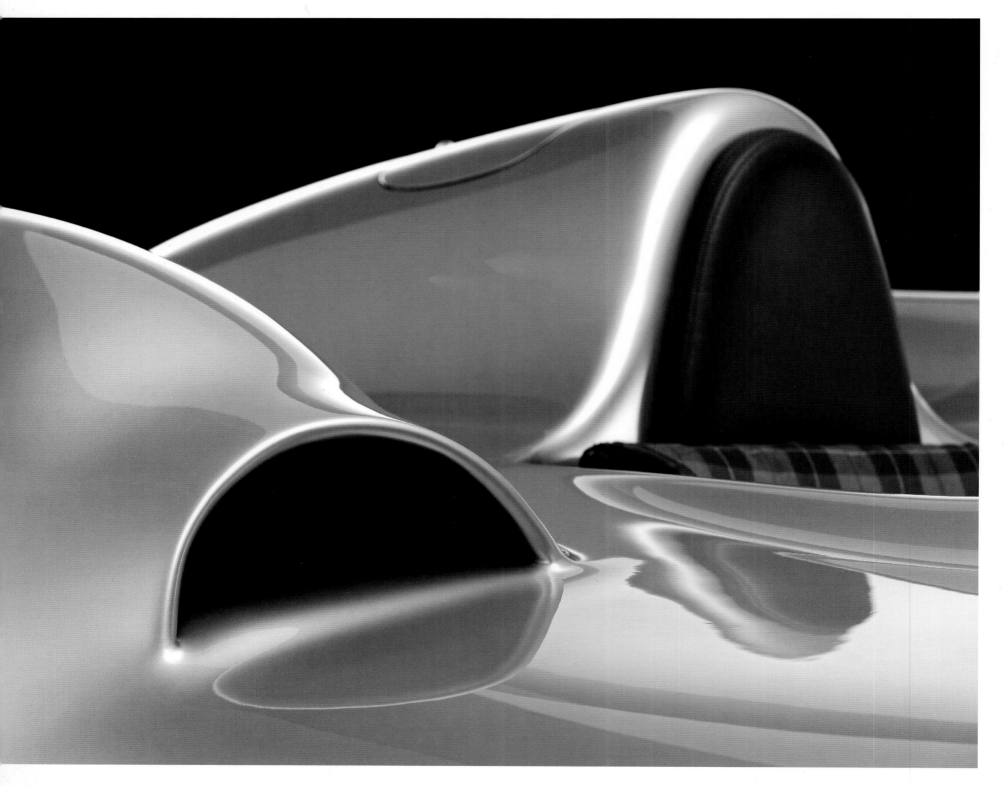

Mercedes-Benz W196

First championship GP
France (Reims), 1954

Last championship GP
Italy (Monza), 1955

Wins/championship races entered
9/12 (3/4 streamlined; 6/9 open-wheel) *

Wins

France (Reims)	1954	Fangio
Germany (Nürburgring)	1954	Fangio **
Switzerland (Bremgarten)	1954	Fangio **
Italy (Monza)	1954	Fangio
Argentina (Buenos Aires)	1955	Fangio **
Belgium (Spa-Francorchamps)	1955	Fangio **
Holland (Zandvoort)	1955	Fangio **
Britain (Silverstone)	1955	Moss **
Italy (Monza)	1955	Fangio

Both types were entered in the 1955 Italian GP.
***Open-wheel model*

Engine
2,496-cc Mercedes-Benz straight eight,
257 horsepower (claimed)

4
Lancia D50

IF THE SECOND COMING OF MERCEDES-BENZ was the most eagerly anticipated event of 1954, the arrival of the Lancia D50 ran it close. Vincenzo Lancia had been a racing driver but never committed his company to the sport; it was his son, Gianni, who spotted an opportunity in the new 2.5-liter Formula 1 rules. He hired Vittorio Jano, designer of the Alfa Romeo 158, to produce a new car, and Alberto Ascari and Luigi Villoresi to drive it. But economics and tragedy would conspire to prevent the car fulfilling its absolute potential.

Throughout the 1954 season, race promoters prayed that they would be blessed with the D50's debut; time and again Lancia declared that it was not yet ready—but would definitely be at the next Grand Prix. The car's repeated non-appearances goaded the specialist press into a frenzy of speculation. The D50 was reported to have been slow in private testing at Monza and kept spinning off the track, even with Ascari at the wheel. Could it have some form of experimental four-wheel-drive system?

Although that particular rumor proved unfounded, the D50 was redolent with fresh thinking, and when it finally appeared in public—a mere ten months late, at the season-closing Spanish Grand Prix at Pedralbes—Ascari demonstrated the car's potential by claiming pole position. In the race, both Lancias retired early with clutch problems, but not before Ascari had stormed away from the pack at a rate of two seconds a lap.

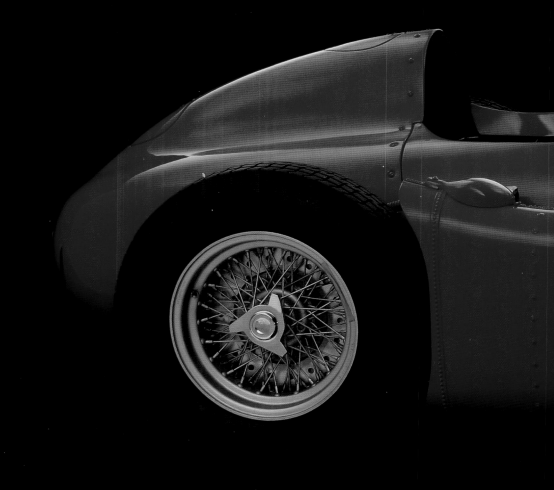

Two-time World Champion Alberto Ascari behind the wheel of the D50 at the 1955 Monaco Grand Prix. This was to be the Italian's last grand prix appearance. After crashing into the harbor during the race, he was killed in a testing crash just two weeks later. LAT Photographic

By the 1956 season, the Ferrari team had faired the gas tanks into the body to improve the car's aerodynamics. Here Juan Manuel Fangio displays his legendary car control on his way to victory at the British Grand Prix at Silverstone. LAT Photographic

The most striking feature of the D50 is the placement of its fuel tanks. In a traditional front-engined F1 car, the only space available to mount the fuel tank was behind the driver—and, therefore, behind the rear axle, where the weight of the fuel would act like a pendulum and swing the tail around mid-corner. Jano hit upon the idea of mounting long panniers on either side of the car to carry the fuel; the design not only improved the weight distribution, but also reduced aerodynamic drag by sealing the gap between the wheels, a gap that would otherwise have been filled with turbulent air. The left-hand pannier also included an oil cooler, although the main oil tank sat behind the driver along with an auxiliary fuel tank.

Jano's other packaging innovation was to reduce overall weight by using the inherent strength of the engine block as part of the chassis structure. Many still credit Lotus' Colin Chapman with introducing this notion to F1, but Jano beat him to it by almost a decade. In effect, the space frame had two principal areas: one built up around the cockpit and rear suspension, and the other around the front suspension; at the

bottom they were connected conventionally, by a long rail on each side, but by bolting the engine securely into the structure the car could go without the upper frame rails. Overall the D50 weighed around 200 kilograms (441 pounds) less than the Mercedes W196 streamliner.

The exceptionally compact 90-degree V-8 enabled the D50 to have a shorter wheelbase than normal, and it was offset so that in combination with a perilously small-diameter driveshaft the driver's seat could be mounted lower in the cockpit. As much of the weight as possible was between the wheels. The result was an agile machine with unparalleled road-holding capabilities, but one that grew twitchy and demanding as it reached its limits of adhesion; the outboard fuel tanks also played a role in dramatically altering the car's handling characteristics as their contents diminished during the course of a race. Where the Maserati 250F would let go with a gentle and predictable slide, the D50 would reach a higher terminal velocity before spinning abruptly—the root, perhaps, of those early rumors that it had four-wheel drive.

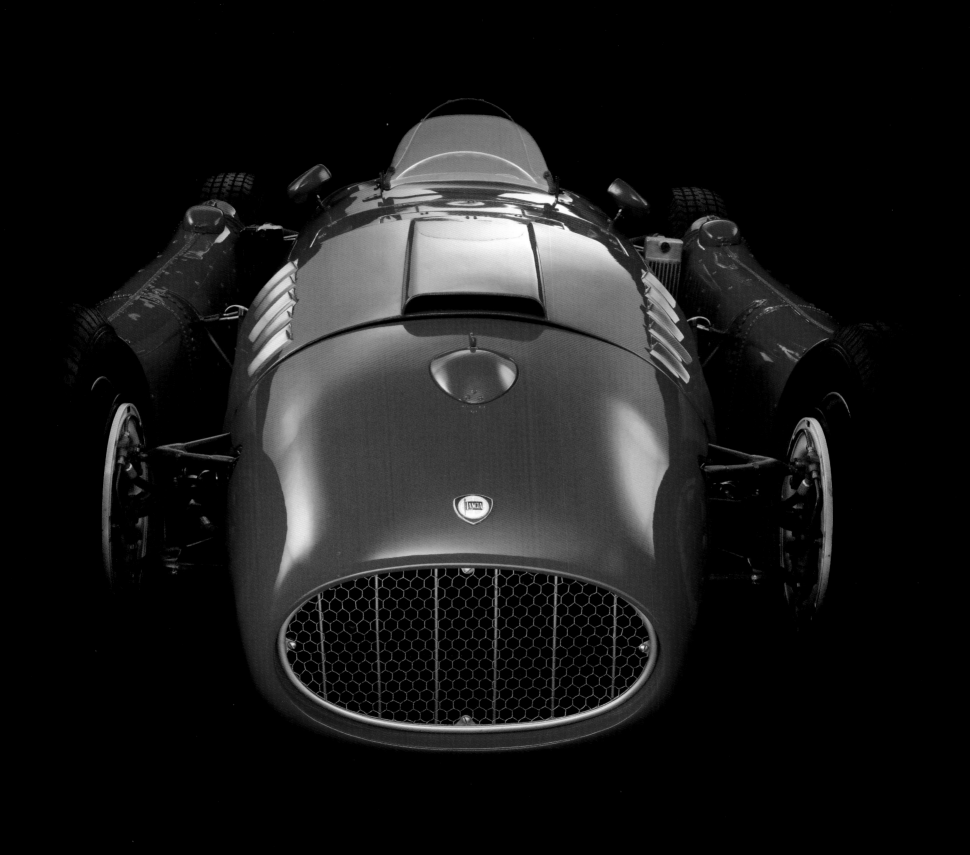

Ascari crashed out while disputing the lead in the first GP of 1955, in Argentina, but he won the non-championship Valentino GP in Turin and finished competitively in two others. The next world championship race was Monaco—where Ascari crashed spectacularly just after assuming the lead, landing in the harbor. A week later, he died in an accident while testing a Ferrari sports car at Monza, and Lancia's F1 dream imploded.

A heavy-hearted Gianni Lancia cancelled the F1 project and put his almost bankrupt company up for sale. Two weeks after the Monaco GP, the field gathered at Spa-Francorchamps for the Belgian GP with just one D50 present—Eugenio Castellotti had begged to be allowed to drive. He put the car on pole position but retired from the race with gearbox failure. The D50's career looked finished—but it was about to be reborn.

A consortium headed by FIAT purchased Lancia and offered Enzo Ferrari a subsidy to take on the D50s. He employed Jano as a consultant but eventually sidelined him to road car projects, while the 1956 season developed into a straight fight for the title between Stirling Moss and two of Ferrari's drivers, Juan Manuel Fangio and Peter Collins. It was Collins who made the decisive move in the final GP of the year at Monza, sportingly pulling in to hand his D50 over to Fangio, who had retired with broken steering.

Ferrari modified the engine and chassis for 1957, renaming it the 801, and making some rather regressive changes to the engineering concept, such as dropping the side-mounted fuel tanks. Fangio jumped ship to Maserati and won the championship; the best Ferrari could manage was a handful of podium finishes, despite having drivers of the caliber of Collins, Mike Hawthorn, and Luigi Musso. It was time for a new model.

All but two of the original D50s were broken up. The car pictured here is one of four beautifully recreated from original parts in the late 1990s with support from collectors, including Donington Park owner Tom Wheatcroft and Formula 1 "ringmaster" Bernie Ecclestone.

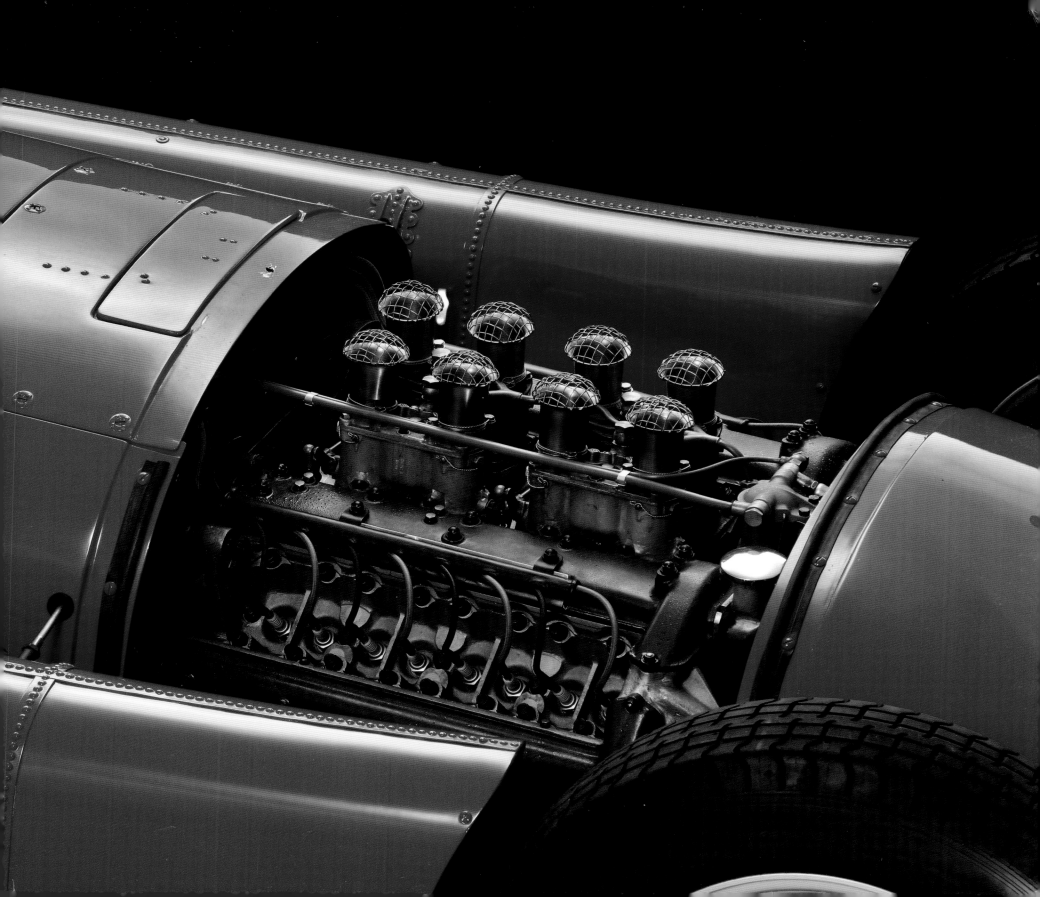

This is my favorite racing car. I've done my own paintings and sketches of it over the years. I love it so much.

It's quite clever in many ways. The polar moment of inertia I'm not so sure about; they've got rid of it front to rear, but increased it sideways by putting the fuel tanks there. Getting the weight of the fuel inside the wheelbase was very difficult to do back then, because you had a long engine bay and a very rear-oriented driving position, so the only place for the fuel was in the tail. So it was clever to get it inside the wheelbase and fair the wheels in as well. And the cars with rear-mounted tanks would have experienced a much bigger change as the fuel load decreased.

Even in those days, the tires would have accounted for a significant proportion of the drag, so cleaning up the turbulence between them would have been an advantage.

Gordon Murray

Lancia D50

First championship GP
Spain (Pedralbes), 1954

Last championship GP
Italy (Monza), 1956

Wins/championship races entered
5/11 *

Wins

Argentina (Buenos Aires)	1956	Musso/ Fangio **
Belgium (Spa-Francorchamps)	1956	Collins
France (Reims)	1956	Collins
Britain (Silverstone)	1956	Fangio
Germany (Nürburgring)	1956	Fangio

Engine
2,496-cc Mercedes-Benz straight eight,
257 horsepower (claimed)

* *Entered 1955 Italian GP but withdrawn*
  after practice.
** *Fangio took over Musso's car.*

5
BRM P57

DURING THE 1950s, THE PHRASE "DOING a BRM" became an accepted comic euphemism in Formula 1 circles for not actually turning up. Founded as a national prestige project by Raymond Mays—a successful driver in the prewar era—and financed by a motor industry consortium, British Racing Motors invested considerable resources in conjuring what is best described as an answer to a question nobody had posed: a 1.5-liter supercharged V-16 engine. It was a typically quirky and quixotic product of British eccentricity, and BRM rapidly acquired the nickname "Team Shambles."

The fabulously complicated V-16 could rarely be persuaded to run reliably—and when it did, its insanely narrow powerband confounded both the drivers and the tire compounds of the day. When results weren't forthcoming, the investors began to drift away. Automotive parts magnate Alfred Owen assumed control, and when F1 became a 2.5-liter formula in 1954, BRM intended to enter with its own chassis and engine. Unfortunately the car wasn't ready in time and the Owen Racing Organisation had to rent a Maserati 250F.

By the time BRM had fettled the P25 into a competitive proposition—Jo Bonnier scored the team's first GP win at Zandvoort in 1959—rear-engined cars were in the ascendant. The team produced a new car for 1960 (designated P48), but it retained several of the pointlessly quirky design features of old (such as a single rear disc brake) and was diabolically

Graham Hill in 1962, the year he joined Mike Hawthorn as the second British World Champion. LAT *Photographic*

Hill demonstrates the P57's agility during the 1963 South African Grand Prix. LAT *Photographic*

unreliable. Drivers Graham Hill and Dan Gurney refused to carry on unless Owen elevated Tony Rudd—who they viewed as the most competent technician in the organization—to oversee all engineering matters.

Rudd's P57 was a competent if conventional machine: lightweight aluminum body panels on a space frame chassis with double-wishbone independent suspension and disc brakes all round. But in true BRM fashion, the new engine for the 1.5-liter formula in 1961 wasn't ready in time, so the team made do with a four-cylinder Coventry Climax in a hybrid P48/57 chassis. In itself this engine was also a stopgap, since Coventry Climax had encountered delays in developing its own V-8.

Hill and Tony Brooks—Gurney had left for Porsche—at last began to finish races, albeit some distance behind the leaders. Meanwhile, Rudd's engineers adapted the chassis (designating it P578) to accommodate the V-8 and a Colotti six-speed gearbox, but after a string of breakages the team reverted to the previous chassis and BRM's own, rather overweight, five-speed transmission. The new engine was utterly conventional in its 90-degree V-8 layout but unusual in its ancillaries: Lucas fuel injection and transistorized ignition, and a dramatic row of megaphone exhausts.

British hillclimb champion Tony Marsh won a non-championship F1 event at Brands Hatch and the P578 ran briefly at the Italian GP, but these efforts were not enough to satisfy Owen, who issued an ultimatum: Win races in 1962 or the team will close.

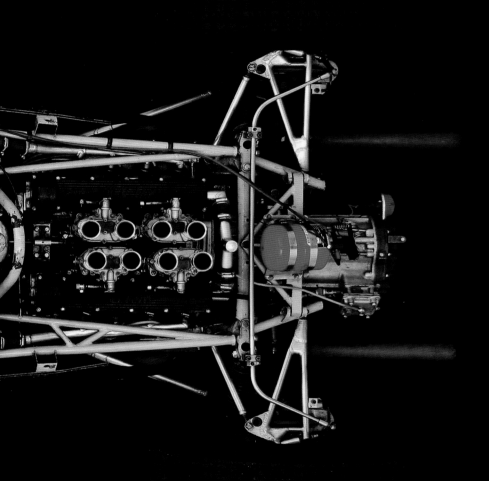

The 1.5-liter era was great for Formula 1, for lots of reasons. You didn't have the power to play with, so you had to get very clever in other areas. It led to all sorts of developments in lighter weight suspension, and eventually the monocoque. Because the engine was so low it allowed the driver to go back to a sort of 30-degree angle, to get the frontal area down and thereby optimize the little power that you had.

Gordon Murray

Over the winter, BRM modified the three existing P57s to accommodate the V-8, with a view to selling them to privateers. The 1962 season began with the non-championship Brussels Grand Prix, held over two heats at a street circuit in the suburb of Heysel. Hill won the first heat, beating the Lotus of Stirling Moss and the works Ferrari of Willy Mairesse. Marsh finished fourth in the P57 photographed here. But the self-starters on both cars failed just before the start of the second heat, and Hill and Marsh were disqualified for receiving push starts. It was a cruel twist: The rules had been changed from the previous year to ban push starts, but the organizers hadn't updated the English translation.

Although the P578 was sporadically troubled by misfires and cooling problems—as well as nagging doubts about whether the V-8 actually attained the power outputs claimed for it—Hill sensed that the championship was his for the taking. Ferrari was in disarray; it was to be between Hill and Jim Clark, driving the stunning Lotus 25. And although Hill's car was heavier and less kind to its tires than Clark's, it was slightly more reliable. And Hill's driving was impeccable that season: At the Nürburgring, he held off a very determined John Surtees and Dan Gurney in abominably wet conditions to take one of the finest victories of his career.

The championship went down to the wire. In the three months between the U.S. GP and the season-closing South African GP on December 29, Rudd looked to pare weight from the P578 while supervising construction of BRM's 1963 car. He had already dispensed with the stackpipe exhausts because they kept breaking off (neither were they aerodynamically efficient). When the car appeared in South Africa, it was indeed lighter than before, but Lotus still won two non-championship races at Kyalami and Westmead, and in the Grand Prix at East London, Clark charged off into an immediate lead, leaving Hill struggling in his wake. Only when Clark pulled in to the pits with an oil leak did the title fall to Hill.

For 1963, BRM redesigned the bottom end of the engine with a flat-plane crank, enabling them to simplify the exhaust system. They also knew that to compete with Lotus they needed the lightness of a monocoque chassis and a new gearbox. But although the new car (dubbed the P61) was considerably lighter, it didn't appear until the Dutch Grand Prix, and then only in practice. It was quick in a straight line but didn't handle; its only race outings came at Reims and Monza. Falling back on the P578, Hill was in with a mathematical shot at the championship until the Italian GP.

BRM's second attempt at a monocoque, the P261, was more successful, and the manufacturer established a lucrative sideline supplying V-8s to customers. But when F1 became a 3-liter formula in 1966, BRM embarked on a disastrous attempt to develop an H-16 engine, which won one race (in the back of a Lotus) but was otherwise overweight and unreliable. And although BRM achieved intermittent successes before finally petering out in 1977, the team never won another championship.

BRM P57

First championship GP
Monaco (Monte Carlo), 1961

Last championship GP
Monaco (Monte Carlo), 1964

Wins/championship races entered
6/28

Wins

Netherlands (Zandvoort)	1962	Hill
Germany (Nürburgring)	1962	Hill
Italy (Monza)	1962	Hill
South Africa (East London)	1962	Hill
Monaco (Monte Carlo)	1963	Hill
U.S. (Watkins Glen)	1963	Hill

Engines
1,498-cc Coventry Climax inline four,
  150 horsepower (est.)
1,498-cc BRM V-8, 190 horsepower (est.)

Note: Owing to BRM's tendency to apply new model designations to chassis that incorporated substantial portions of existing cars, the results presented here run from the first outing of the P48/57 to the final race of the P578.

"The mechanics and packaging of this car are so well-done; it's all been kept very small. And it's very pretty."

Gordon Murray

6

Brabham BT20

JACK BRABHAM WAS ONE OF THOSE drivers who had an instinctive understanding of engineering principles. At the beginning of his racing career, in Australia, he built his own cars. Later, after winning two Formula 1 World Championships for Cooper in 1959 and 1960, he then set out to become the first racing driver to win a championship in a Grand Prix in a car he'd made himself.

Brabham persuaded his old friend Ron Tauranac to leave Australia and go into partnership with him. Working under the deliberately nondescript name of Motor Racing Developments Ltd., Tauranac began designing cars for lower formulae in secret while Brabham continued to drive for Cooper. At the end of 1961, Brabham quit Cooper and entered the championship under his own name for 1962, initially fielding a customer Lotus until the first Brabham F1 car was ready.

Since Brabham was unwilling to sink too much of his own money into the project, MRD's principal financial stream came from selling cars to private entrants. As such, the F1 project initially struggled for lack of resources, and Tauranac continued to build space frame chassis long after other manufacturers had switched to monocoques, firm in his belief that a properly designed space frame was just as good.

At first, Tauranac concentrated on MRD's business; Brabham's racing team operated as a separate entity and bought chassis from MRD like any other

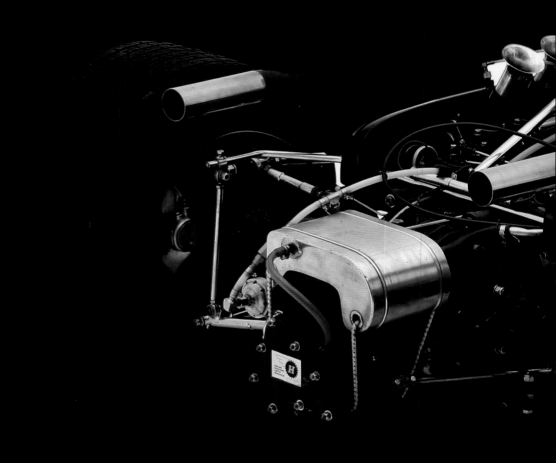

customer. In private, Tauranac had reservations about the arrangement and reportedly was unhappy with the amount of credit Brabham was taking for the design of the cars. Dan Gurney won two championship Grands Prix in 1964, but otherwise the results were thin. At the end of 1965, Brabham and Tauranac arrived at a rapprochement, giving Tauranac a greater role in F1 operations; this move coincided with one of the formula's periodic rules upheavals.

F1 was due to become a 3-liter formula in 1966, and the majority of engine manufacturers had invested their time in lobbying against the change rather than tooling up for it. Just as they had done before the switch to 1.5-liter engines in 1961, many teams appeared to take the view that if they ignored the matter it would go away. But Brabham had found a willing engine partner: the Australian automotive parts specialist, Repco.

Initially built in 2.5-liter form for Brabham's use in the Tasman series, the Repco engine was a clever and resourceful mishmash of mostly off-the-shelf parts. Repco produced the cylinder heads, the connecting rods were from the Daimler parts bin, and the cam followers came from Alfa Romeo. The blocks were remnants from Oldsmobile's attempt to build an all-aluminum engine for its road car range; after innumerable problems with quality and

Lots of cars at the time had inboard suspension—for aerodynamic reasons—and it was horrible. The rocker arms were so floppy they basically acted like un-damped springs. Having proper suspension geometry gave a handling advantage that probably outweighed the small drag penalty of having the springs in the airflow.

Gordon Murray

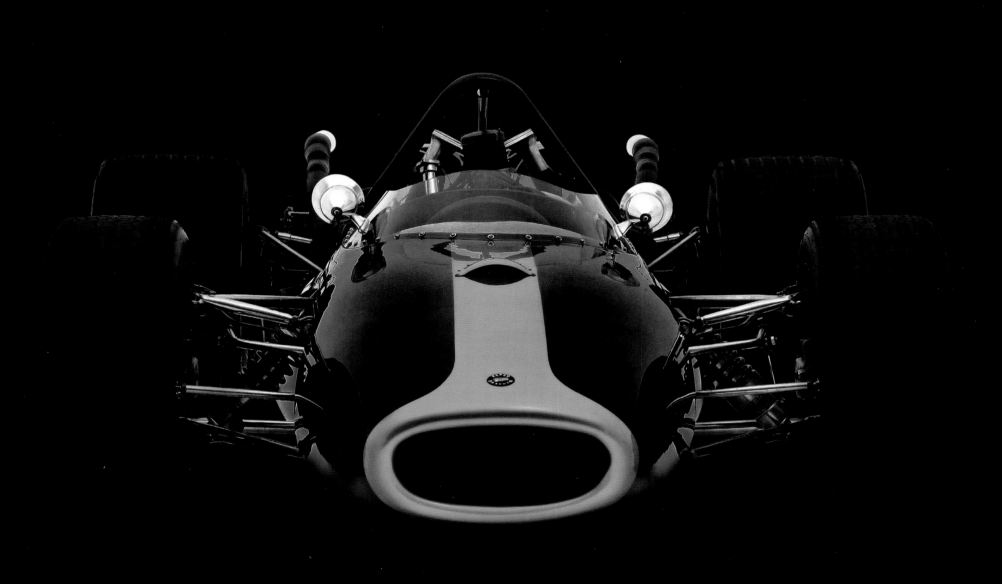

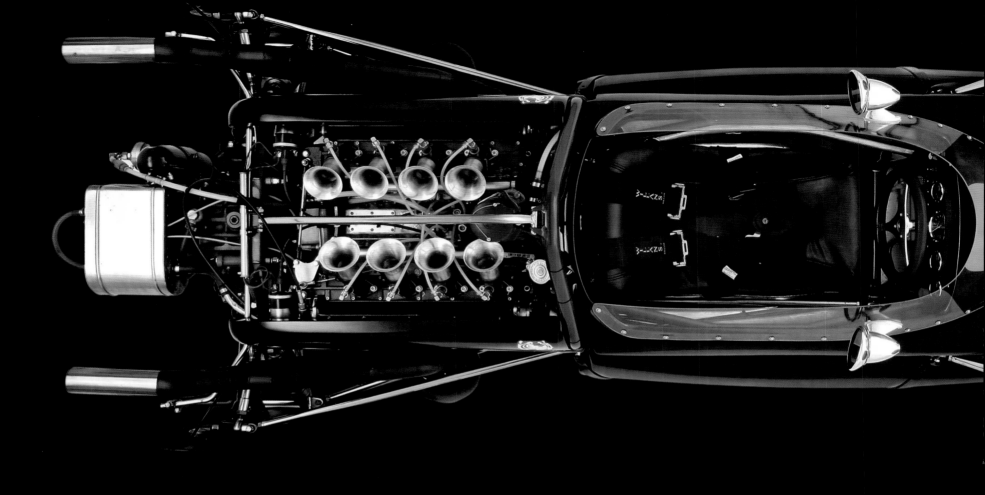

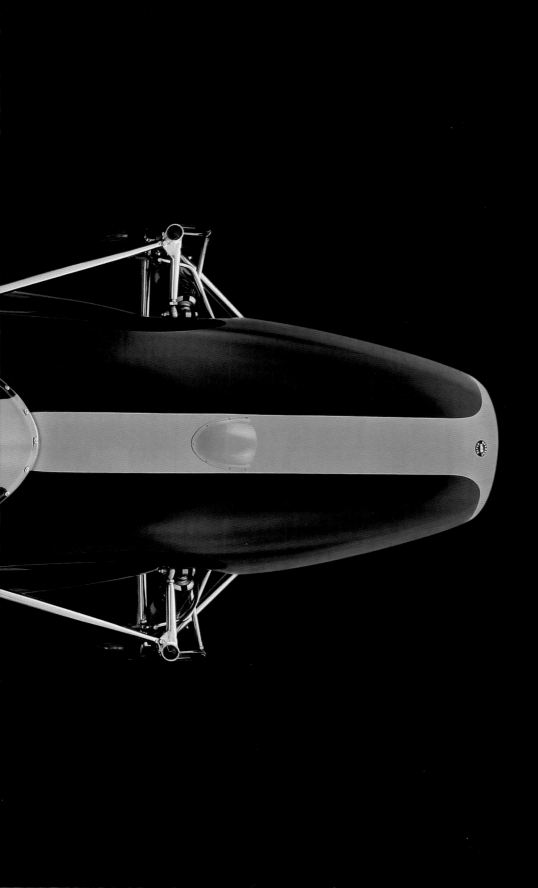

consistency in the casting process, General Motors had abandoned the design and sold off the remaining stock. As a 3-liter race engine it made 300 horsepower, which was adequate, if not up to Ferrari standards. But it was impressively torquey.

The early months of 1966 were a mad rush for the teams that had been caught napping by the regulation change. Cooper resorted to a Maserati V-12 that had been sitting on the shelf for the best part of a decade (it had originally been designed to go in the 250F toward the end of its life). Tauranac hadn't had enough time to build an all-new car to accommodate the Repco engine, so he slotted the V-8 into an existing chassis that he had designed for the putative Climax flat-16 at the end of 1964.

The BT19 may have been a product of expediency rather than a thoroughly integrated design, but it was nimble and well balanced. The shape was a product of wind-tunnel research, but Tauranac had resisted the temptation to mount the springs inside the chassis and out of the airflow; the double-wishbone setup was stiffer and offered better geometry than rocker arms. Allied to the Repco engine's driver-friendly spread of torque, the BT19 was a useful car; Brabham's teammate, Denny Hulme, soldiered on with the aged BT11 (powered by a 2.7-liter Climax engine) during the opening races of the season.

Brabham's gearbox failed in Monaco—the Hewland transmission was designed for 2-liter engines and not quite robust enough for 300 horsepower—and he finished fourth in the wet and anarchic Belgian GP at Spa-Francorchamps. At Reims, the third race of the year, the new BT20 was ready—just about. Brabham decided to stick with the BT19—the "Old Nail" as he called it—leaving Hulme to race the first BT20, which the team finished assembling in the paddock on the Thursday night. Lorenzo Bandini qualified his Ferrari on pole by a comfortable margin, but when his throttle cable snapped in the race, Brabham sailed into the lead and stayed there. He was the first person to win a championship Grand Prix in a car bearing his own name. Hulme finished

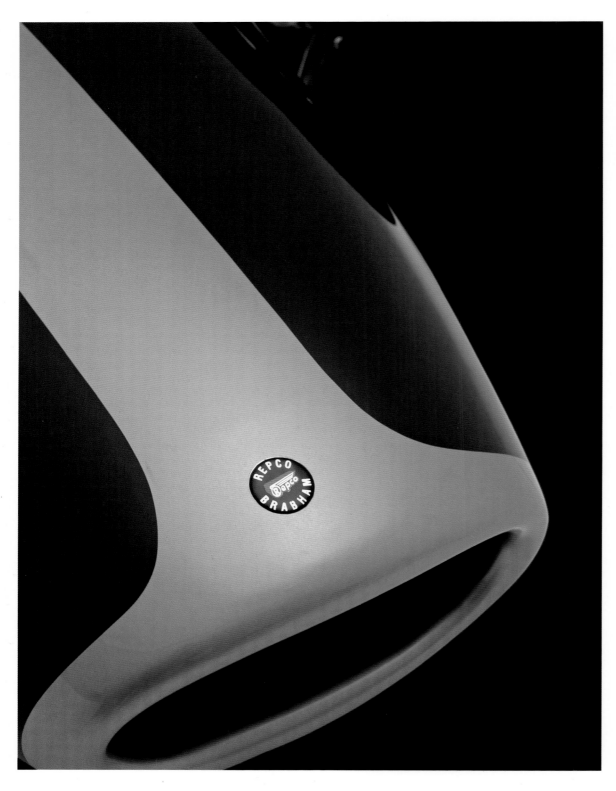

third, despite having to stop and lift the front of his car to cure a fuel-feed problem.

The BT20 was a rigorous evolution of the BT19, longer in the wheelbase and more torsionally stiff. Tauranac also fitted bigger brakes to cope with the power of the engine and the extra weight of the up-rated chassis. But Brabham felt more comfortable in the lighter BT19; race after race, as the 1966 season wore on, he would opt for the "Old Nail." He won three more championship GPs in it, followed by the International Gold Cup at Oulton Park in the U.K., before swapping to the BT20 for the last two races of the season. He set pole at Watkins Glen before retiring with engine failure, then finished second to John Surtees in Mexico.

At 40 years of age—and a year after speaking of possible retirement—Jack Brabham had won his third world championship, this time in a car bearing his own name. Australia had beaten the world.

But the aftermath of this success would reveal tensions in the organization. Tauranac was always uncomfortable with the amount of credit the press gave to Brabham for the design of the cars; and the relationship with Repco, always difficult given the physical distance between the U.K. and Australia, also turned sour over the issue of who deserved credit for what.

In any case, the new Cosworth engine's power output massively outclassed the Repco's. Denny Hulme won the 1967 championship for Brabham (including victory at the Monaco GP in chassis BT20-2, photographed here, before switching to the new BT24), but he did so largely because the much quicker Lotus 49 driven by Jim Clark and Graham Hill kept breaking down.

At the end of 1968, Repco decided that F1 was too expensive and withdrew, leaving Brabham to join the Cosworth club. The team had achieved little that year, but its new driver, Jochen Rindt, had brought with him from Cooper a young mechanic who in later years would play an enormous role in the sport: Ron Dennis.

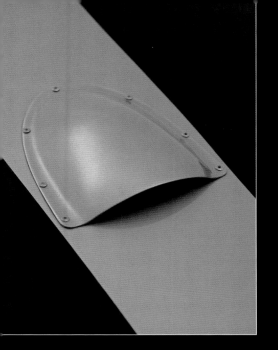

Ron Tauranac (left) and Jack Brabham (center) in 1967. LAT Photographic

Brabham BT20

First championship GP
France (Reims), 1966

Last championship GP
South Africa (Kyalami), 1969

Wins/championship races entered
1/22

Wins
Monaco (Monte Carlo)   1967   Hulme

Engine
2,994-cc Repco V-8, 300 horsepower (est.)

1967 Monaco Grand Prix. Denny Hulme, protuberant tongue and all, flies down the waterfront en route to his and the BT20's first Formula 1 victories. LAT Photographic

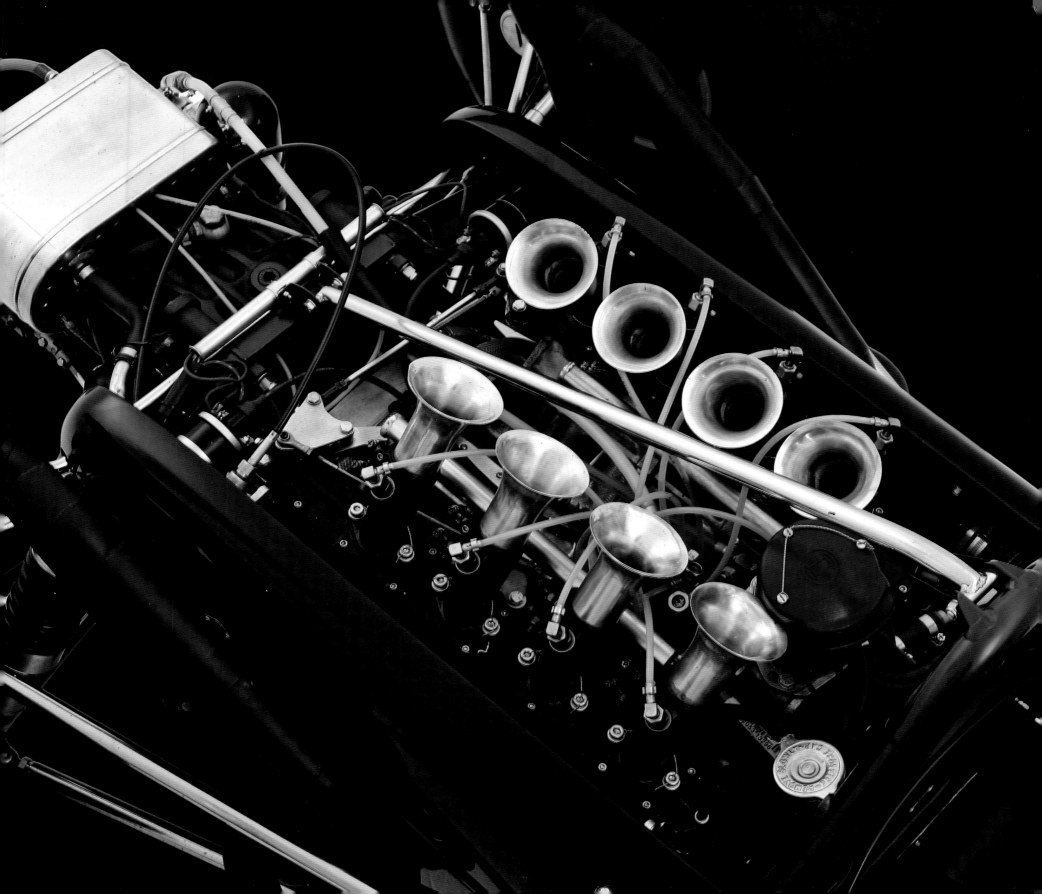

7

Lotus 49B

DURING THE 1960s, TWO CHANGES TO the Formula 1 engine regulations were to have profound consequences on the sport. In finding the best way to exploit the new rules, Colin Chapman's Lotus team would lead F1 design in a direction from which it has scarcely deviated in four decades.

The move to 1.5-liter engines in 1961 put a premium on efficiency, and Lotuses were at the forefront: Chapman rendered the space frame obsolete in 1962 with the Lotus 25, a monocoque design in which the majority of the body panels formed a structural part of the chassis with integrated fuel tanks on either side of the driver. Chapman also returned to a principle first explored in F1 by Vittorio Jano on the Lancia D50: reducing overall weight by using the engine block to take some of the suspension loads. The 25 was a sleekly minimalist missile that through ruthless weight-saving overcame the obstacle of its underpowered Coventry Climax engine. In 1963, the peerless Jim Clark won seven out of the ten Grands Prix in it, taking Lotus' first drivers' and constructors' championships.

Clark won the drivers' title again in 1965, but for the following season the maximum permitted engine size doubled to 3 liters, leaving the manufacturers facing a quandary. Several even threatened to pull out. Lotus went with BRM, which offered the solution to flatten the "vee" of its 1.5-liter V-8 and mate two back to back with a shared crankshaft, forming an H-16. The block was strong enough for Lotus to use

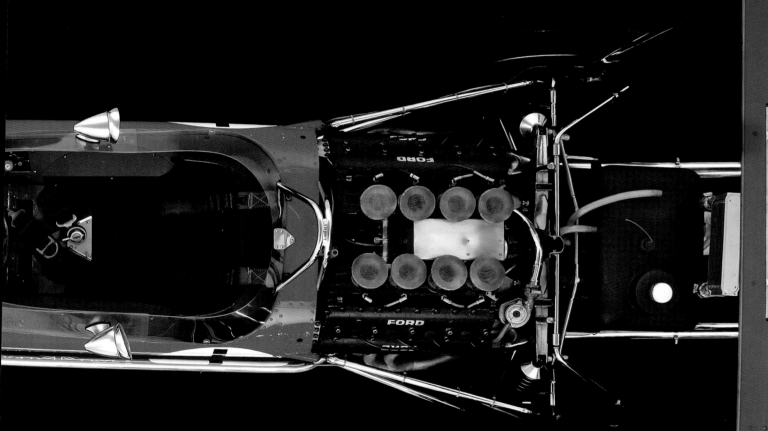

it as a fully stressed member of the chassis, taking the principle Jano had explored at Lancia to its logical conclusion: The "tub" would end with a bulkhead behind the driver and the engine would bolt onto it, with the suspension bearing off it and the gearbox. It was vastly overweight, though, and—with valve gear more intricate than a Swiss timepiece—too complicated to be reliable. Clark was able to drive the H-16-powered Lotus 43 to victory at the U.S. GP at Watkins Glen, but by then Chapman had begun to look elsewhere for power for his 1967 car. He persuaded Walter Hayes of Ford to bankroll a bespoke 3-liter V-8 designed and built by Cosworth.

The Lotus-Cosworth 49 was quick—claiming pole position in 10 consecutive Grands Prix—but not reliable enough, and Denny Hulme won the 1967 championship in the relatively old-fashioned (it had a space frame chassis) Brabham BT24. Cosworth, having demonstrated the potency of its engine, was going to supply other teams as well in 1968, so Lotus urgently needed to find reliability as well as refine the 49's performance.

Meanwhile, there was another revolution brewing in aerodynamics. F1 designers had long understood the virtues of giving their cars a clean profile to achieve maximum straight-line speed. By the mid-1960s, they were beginning to look at another way of exploiting the airflow—to boost cornering speeds and solve handling imbalances. Enzo Ferrari demonstrated the potential of spoilers on his sports cars, and by 1968 F1 cars were also sprouting slim, aluminum aero appendages.

These would not be the only changes to the look of F1 cars that year. When the 1968 season began, the factory Lotus 49s caused outrage by running in the colors of their new sponsor, Gold Leaf tobacco, rather than their traditional British Racing Green. Although rocked by Clark's death in an F2 race at Hockenheim in April, the team brought out the 49B in time for Monaco, with a marginally narrower monocoque, fins on each side of the nose, and an upswept tail section. Making a slight concession to driver comfort, the team transferred the oil tank and cooler to the rear (in a neat saddle-tank arrangement over the gearbox to avoid upsetting the weight distribution) so that hot oil wasn't being piped along the sides of the cockpit. Graham Hill found the new car a massive advance over the old—the updated suspension geometry cured it of its tendency to be knocked off course by bumps—and duly became the first person to win the Monaco GP four times.

The only retrograde element of the 49B came about as a result of switching from a ZF gearbox to the Hewland FG400, which wasn't strong enough to take the full suspension load and required a small crossmember at the rear. But it enabled the team to swap gear ratios without stripping the entire unit, which made the 49B a considerably more practical car to work on during a race weekend.

Other teams sprinted to follow Lotus' lead. Two weeks after Monaco, a host of cars arrived at Spa-Francorchamps sporting new fins. But Chapman was moving the game on. Every time the 49B appeared, it had some new aerodynamic refinement. The ducktail bodywork gave way to an aero foil—rather like a scaled-down model of an upside-down

Reliability issues robbed Jim Clark of the championship in 1967. But he opened the 1968 season with a resounding win at Kyalami, taking pole and fastest lap in the process. This would be his final Formula 1 race, the last in which the 49 would be seen in British Racing Green. LAT Photographic

Graham Hill behind the wheel of Lotus 49B, chassis number R6, in one of its many iterations: nose fins and a tall aerofoil mounted to the rear suspension. Classic Team Lotus

aircraft wing—mounted on aluminum pillars bearing off the hub carriers, they sat high above the car in clear air. Soon everyone was at it. Following the example of the Chaparral Can-Am car, Lotus fitted high front wings, also mounted on the hub carriers via a perilously slim piece of aluminum on each side. Hill rode the wave and clinched the championship at the final round, driving the car pictured here, chassis R6.

That summer, there had been a string of fatal accidents in motor racing, including four F1 drivers. The authorities grew nervous and some drivers—led by the voluble Jackie Stewart—began to complain about lax safety provisions at the circuits and on the cars. None of this stopped the teams from chasing downforce through the use of high wings. Hill was shocked to discover at the first race of the 1969 season that everyone now had high wings—and they were breaking frighteningly often.

Hill's new teammate, Jochen Rindt, set the pace in the second GP of the season, the first time Montjuich Park in Barcelona had hosted a Grand Prix since the 1930s. On the ninth lap, Hill's rear wing sheared off as he crested a rise and he speared off into the barrier, emerging shaken but unhurt. Eleven laps later, Rindt's wing failed in exactly the same place, and he hurtled at barely diminished speed into the wreckage of his teammate's car. Rindt was lucky to survive with just a broken nose to show for it. The high wings were banned in short order.

The 49B gradually slipped from competitiveness as Chapman diverted all his resources into ultimately fruitless gas turbine and four-wheel-drive projects. Hill won again in Monaco, but that would be the team's only victory of the year. The car that had brought wings and tobacco sponsorship into F1 would see in the new decade, racing in the first Grands Prix of 1970s in "C" spec before its replacement was finally ready. The engine that had been built for it would carry on powering F1 winners for years to come.

*The rear wing stays look flimsy, but it
would only have been inertial force pushing
it sideways—if the rear wheels let go and
gripped again. It would only get dodgy if
you'd done your sums wrong and you were
near the buckling load on the strut; then, if
you got inertial force, it could bend the strut
and you'd get a collapse. Obviously, if you
could get away with it, you'd aim to have
the downforce acting on the unsprung part of
the car so it wasn't using up valuable wheel
travel through the spring. They eventually
changed the rules so that anything having an
aerodynamic effect had to be on an entirely
sprung part of the car.*

Gordon Murray

Lotus 49

First championship GP
Netherlands (Zandvoort), 1967

Last championship GP
U.S. (Watkins Glen), 1970

Wins/championship races entered
11/42

Wins

Netherlands (Zandvoort)	1967	Hill
Great Britain (Silverstone)	1967	Clark
U.S. (Watkins Glen)	1967	Clark
Mexico (Mexico City)	1967	Clark
South Africa (Kyalami)	1968	Clark
Monaco (Monte Carlo)	1968	Hill
Great Britain (Brands Hatch)	1968	Jo Siffert
Mexico (Mexico City)	1968	Hill
Monaco (Monte Carlo)	1969	Hill
U.S. (Watkins Glen)	1969	Rindt
Monaco (Monte Carlo)	1969	Rindt

Engine
2,993-cc Ford-Cosworth V-8, 430 horsepower (est.)

8

Lotus 72

PERHAPS THE SEMINAL FORMULA 1 CAR
of the early 1970s, the Lotus 72 enjoyed a remarkably
long term of service given the rapid advances of
the time. In all, it would contest six seasons—long
outstaying its golden period, but only because Lotus
once again out-thought itself in trying to develop a
suitably advanced replacement for it.

Through plowing considerable time and
resources into developing a four-wheel-drive chassis
and then, after that failed to be competitive, a car
that could accommodate a gas turbine engine, Lotus'
engineering mastermind Colin Chapman had allowed
the Type 49 to become very long in the tooth. By
1970, Lotus was desperate for a replacement. The 72
was the work of Maurice Phillippe, and while little
of it was individually revolutionary, it was a neat and
modern-looking package.

Unveiled to the world's press in Gold Leaf livery at
Lotus' factory early in 1970, the Cosworth-powered 72
had a pronounced wedge profile with more integrated
wings than its predecessor. To reduce unsprung
weight and enable the team to use softer-compound
tires, the brake discs were mounted inboard—cooling
air flowed in through a pair of NACA ducts and then
exited through small chimneys on the nose. Phillippe
also relocated the water radiators from the nose to
the sidepods to improve weight distribution. This
wasn't the first time it had been done in F1, but soon
everyone followed Lotus' example, making this the
default location.

The suspension was a complicated torsion bar arrangement, intended to prevent the car from diving under braking and squatting under acceleration. The suspension was to be the root of most of the 72's early problems; there were a number of structural failures in testing, and the drivers complained that the geometry robbed them of "feel." The 72's race debut—in Spain, the second Grand Prix of the year—was little short of a disaster. John Miles failed to qualify and Jochen Rindt retired, while Graham Hill finished fourth in a privately entered 49C. Chapman withdrew the 72 for more development, and Rindt entered the next two races in the venerable 49C, winning in Monaco.

When it emerged that the drivers could lap as quickly (or quicker) without the anti-dive and anti-squat suspension, Lotus changed to a more conventional system. But there were other problems: The chassis was flexing and had to be beefed up, at the cost of adding a little weight. At the British GP, the team arrived with another innovation: a scoop mounted over the engine to direct extra air in, boosting power. Rindt won the race, his third of four consecutive victories that summer, and he entered the final phase of the season with an almost insurmountable championship lead.

Then, at Monza, the team suffered a crushing blow. Rindt went out for a practice run without wings to see if the 72 could better its lap time in low-drag form. As he applied the brakes before the Parabolica corner, his car slid violently off the track and into a barrier. Rindt was pronounced dead on arrival at the hospital. There wasn't enough of the car left intact to arrive at a definitive explanation for the accident, although it is most likely that a shaft connected to one of the front brake discs sheared. It subsequently emerged that bolts holding the safety barrier together had rusted, causing it to fail under the impact. If the barrier had held, he might have survived. As it was, Rindt became F1's only posthumous champion.

Firestone's new family of low-profile tires for the 1971 season didn't suit the 72 at all—they generated so much grip that the suspension was distorting

Colin Chapman (in hat) and Jochen Rindt confer during the 1970 Dutch Grand Prix weekend at Zandvoort, where Rindt would pilot the 72 to its first victory. Ron Easton/LAT Photographic

under load. It took Lotus all year to identify and cure the problem, by which time their lead driver, Emerson Fittipaldi, had grown disaffected. And, by dint of being not quite as quick as Fittipaldi in a difficult car, their number two Reine Wisell barely figured.

A change to Goodyear tires proved to be the remedy and, together with the new John Player Special livery, the 1972 season felt like a fresh start for the beleaguered team. Fittipaldi swept to the drivers' championship, utterly dominating his teammate Dave Walker, a young Australian who had won the 1971 British Formula 3 championship for Lotus.

The 1973 iteration, the 72E, was the definitive 72, with the sidepods modified to incorporate the new mandatory crash structure. Ironically, Chapman's decision to give Fittipaldi a more competitive teammate would leave Lotus holding only the constructors' championship: Fittipaldi won three races but "Super Swede" Ronnie Peterson won four, handing the drivers' title to Jackie Stewart.

Feeling upstaged, Fittipaldi left for McLaren. Lotus had been working on a new car, the 76, which was essentially a lighter development of the 72 with different aerodynamics, and an electronic clutch (operated via the gear stick) to facilitate quicker shifting. But the new gear change was problematic, and the car's weight distribution was fundamentally wrong for the new generation of tires, forcing Lotus to run Peterson and Jacky Ickx in 72s for the majority of 1974. Peterson was in the running for the championship, but Chapman was so determined to make the 76 work that he neglected the 72, which in any case was verging on obsolete after five seasons.

After finally giving up on the 76, the team ran the 72 throughout 1975, continually modifying the suspension to little effect; the new, harder-compound tires required a more forward-biased weight distribution that couldn't be achieved without adding ballast or producing an entirely new car—which is what Lotus eventually did, pioneering innovative aerodynamics with a stunning return to form at the end of the decade.

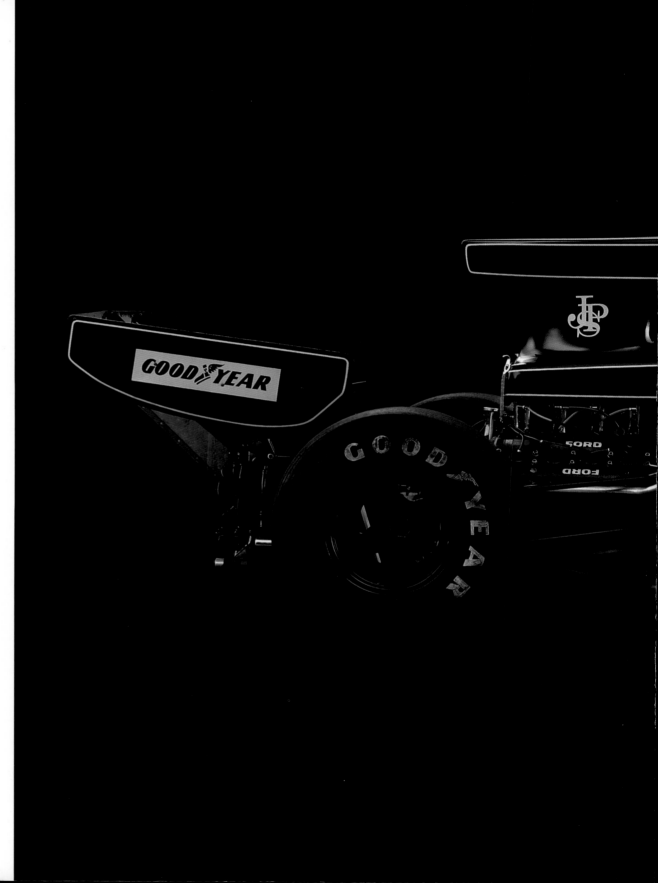

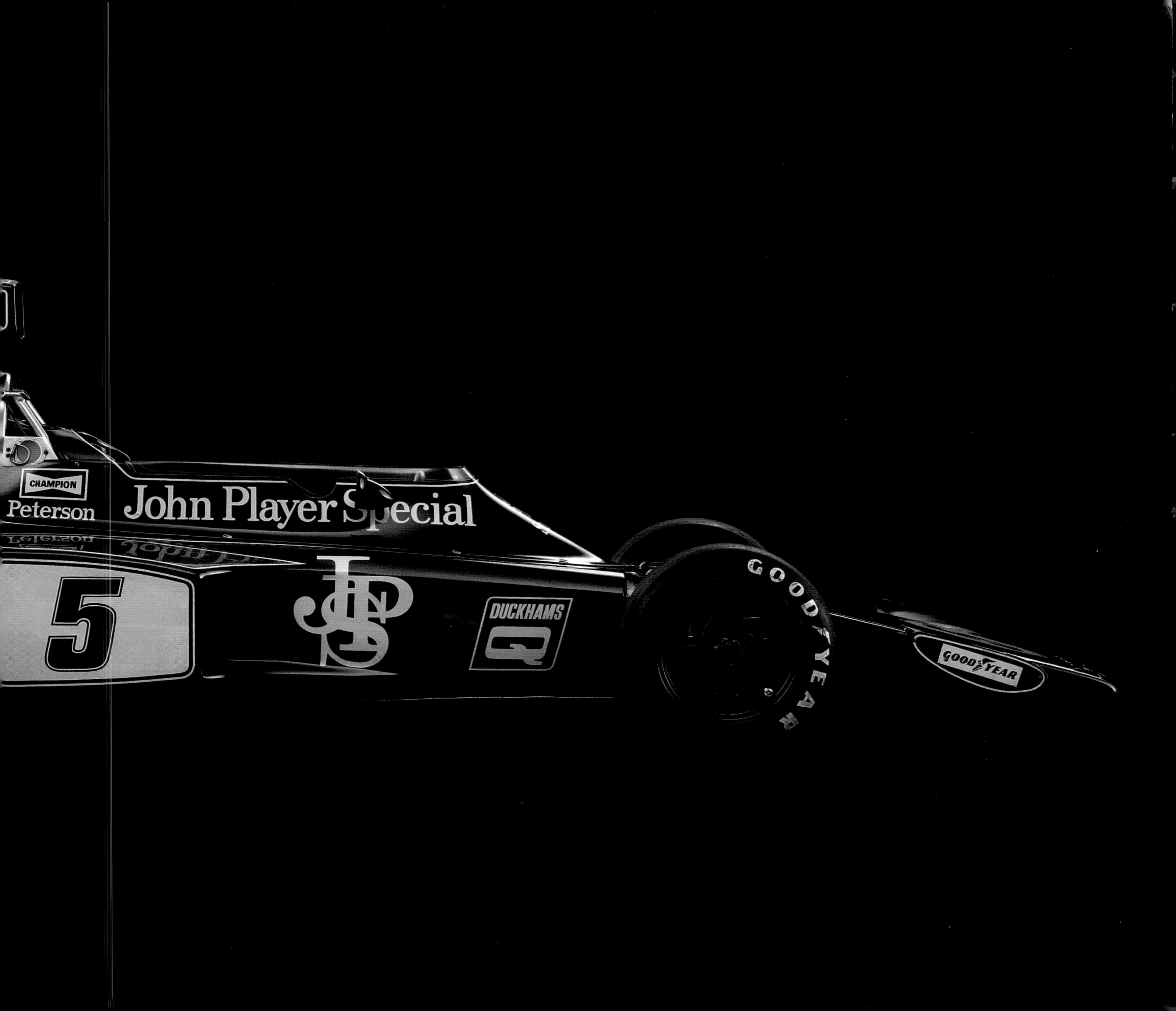
CHAMPION
Peterson
John Player Special
5
DUCKHAMS
GOODYEAR
GOODYEAR

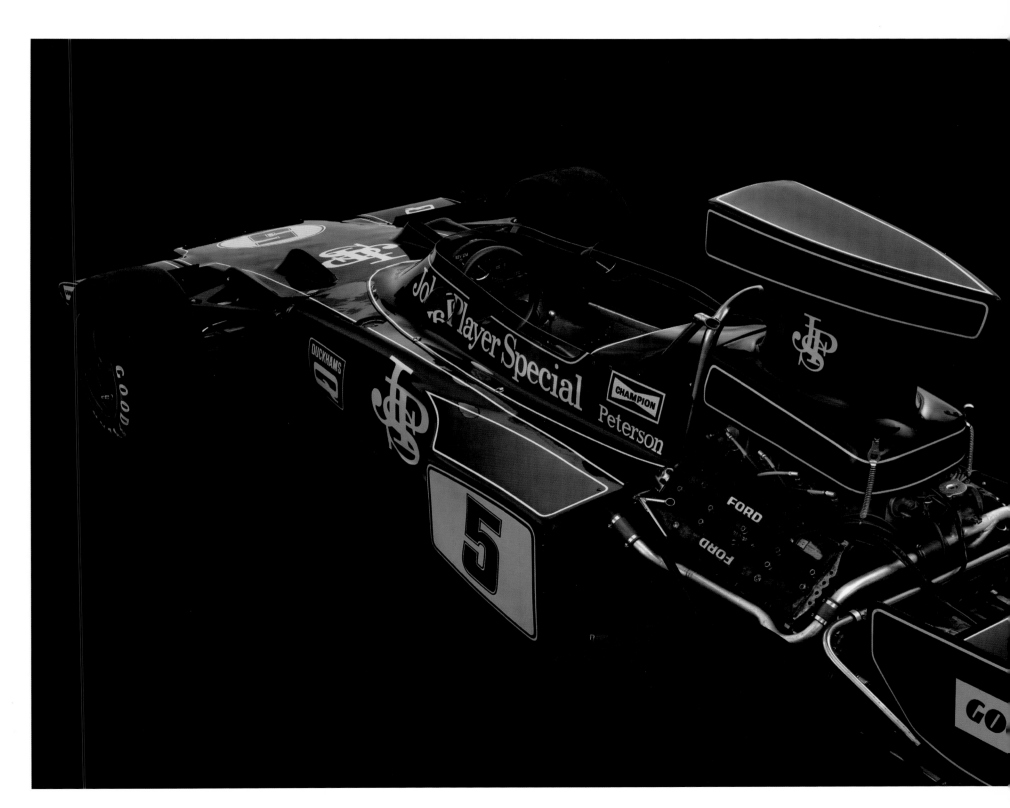

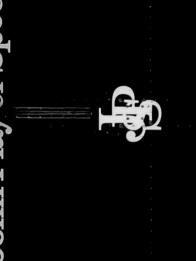
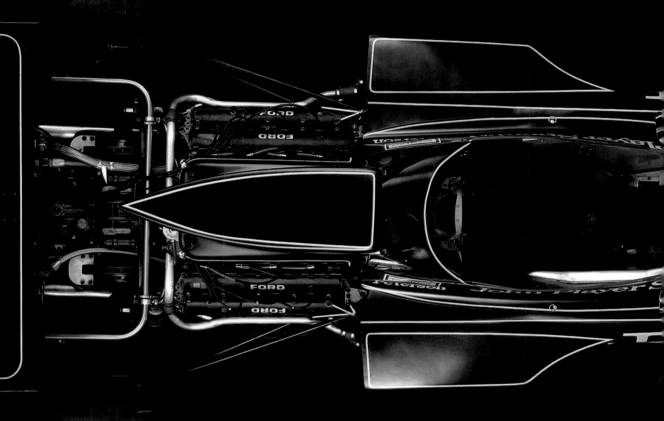

Emerson Fittipaldi scored 9 of his 14 Formula 1 championship wins in the Lotus 72. Classic Team Lotus

"The biggest step forward from an aerodynamics point of view was the skinny, low nose and side-mounted radiators. A lot of the cars had front radiators before that. All the other innovation was hidden in the chassis. Technically it was ahead of its time. I liked the fact that they were trying inboard brakes; that would have come from Colin's experiments with four-wheel drive, I suppose. Whenever I took a big step forward in F1 it was always to do with the fundamentals, such as the center of gravity or the center of pressure, or something with the aerodynamics. Whereas Chapman tended to say, 'Right, I want inboard brakes, so I'll do a layout that suits inboard brakes.' He focused on one or two innovations rather than the holistic thing. I came from a different background; I'd look around and think, say, 'All the other cars have a weight distribution that changes by two percent during the race, wouldn't it be great for our drivers if ours only changed by one percent?'"

Gordon Murray

Lotus 72

First championship GP
Spain (Jarama), 1970

Last championship GP
U.S. (Watkins Glen), 1975

Wins/championship races entered
20/76

Wins

Netherlands (Zandvoort)	1970	Rindt
France (Clermont-Ferrand)	1970	Rindt
Great Britain (Brands Hatch)	1970	Rindt
Germany (Hockenheim)	1970	Rindt
U.S. (Watkins Glen)	1970	Fittipaldi
Spain (Jarama)	1972	Fittipaldi
Belgium (Nivelles)	1972	Fittipaldi
Great Britain (Brands Hatch)	1972	Fittipaldi
Austria (Österreichring)	1972	Fittipaldi
Italy (Monza)	1972	Fittipaldi
Argentina (Buenos Aires)	1973	Fittipaldi
Brazil (Interlagos)	1973	Fittipaldi
Spain (Montjuich Park)	1973	Fittipaldi
France (Paul Ricard)	1973	Peterson
Austria (Österreichring)	1973	Peterson
Italy (Monza)	1973	Peterson
U.S. (Watkins Glen)	1973	Peterson
Monaco (Monte Carlo)	1974	Peterson
France (Dijon)	1974	Peterson
Italy (Monza)	1974	Peterson

Engine
3,993-cc Ford-Cosworth V-8, 440 horsepower (est.)

9
Tyrrell 003

FOR A BRIEF PERIOD IN THE EARLY 1970s, the Formula 1 team everyone wanted to beat was a family business run with contagious enthusiasm by a former timber merchant. Ken Tyrrell—once nicknamed "Chopper"—ran a tight ship. Even when the team was riding high with prominent backing from Ford and Elf, visitors to the Tyrrell factory would be surprised to find that it consisted of three sheds and some Portakabins; indeed, its first self-built car was designed in utmost secrecy by a former aeronautics engineer in his bedroom.

Tyrrell had not set out to build his own car. It was his dream to compete in F1, and he had arrived there by running bought-in chassis through Formula Junior, F3, and F2 in the 1960s, cultivating a reputation for discovering young talent. It was in these lower formulae that he met the outstanding Jackie Stewart, who won the British F3 championship for him in 1964.

Through the motor racing journalist Jabby Crombac, Tyrrell was introduced to Elf, the French petrochemicals giant, and Matra, the French aerospace corporation that built cars as a sideline. Tyrrell entered F1 in 1968 as Equipe Matra International with an Elf-liveried, Cosworth V-8-powered Matra MS9 for Stewart, later expanding to a second car for Johnny Servoz-Gavin. It was a typically low-key effort: Just 10 staff went to a Grand Prix, including Tyrrell's wife, Norah, who sat on the pit wall and kept the lap charts.

An unbeatable duo: Ken Tyrrell (left) and Jackie Stewart would pair to win three drivers' and two constructors' championships from 1969 to 1973. *LAT Photographic*

Another unbeatable pairing: Stewart behind the wheel of Tyrrell 003 at the Nürburgring in 1972. *LAT Photographic*

Stewart flew once he was installed in the newer MS10 chassis, even though he wore a brace for much of the 1968 season after fracturing a bone in his wrist. He won the drivers' title with the MS80 in 1969, but by then a schism was developing between Matra and Tyrrell: Matra had developed its own V-12 engine with Elf money and was determined to use it. Tyrrell was equally determined to stay with Ford power. The partnership dissolved.

Tyrrell bought a March 701 chassis and entered the 1970 F1 season as the Tyrrell Racing Organisation, but both he and Stewart rapidly became disenchanted with the March's indifferent performance and lack of development potential. He resolved to design and build his own car in secret. Stewart recalls their conversation in his autobiography:

"I'm tired of relying on other people and being disappointed," said Tyrrell.

"Can you afford it?"

"I think so."

Tyrrell engaged Derek Gardner, a former aerospace engineer with motorsports experience, to design a car. To preserve secrecy, Gardner worked from the bedroom of his house in Leamington Spa. In August 1970, Tyrrell unveiled the 001 to the abject surprise of the world media, followed by a competitive outing in the nonchampionship Oulton Park Gold Cup, where it suffered fueling problems. Stewart continued to race the March chassis until the 001's bugs had been ironed out; when it was finally ready, at the end of September, he put the 001 on pole at the Canadian GP and led until an axle failed.

The 001 was handsome and quick but not quite reliable enough. Over the winter of 1970, Gardner refined his designs and produced two new chassis: 002 for Stewart's new teammate, François Cevert, and 003 for Stewart. At this stage, Tyrrell named his cars individually rather than by chassis type.

Stewart likened the 003 to a thoroughbred racehorse. It was quick, robust, and responsive to setup changes. Gardner had lengthened the wheelbase slightly, making it less twitchy, and altered the nose and monocoque to create a more slippery profile. When Stewart got in the 003 for its first race, the Spanish GP at Montjuich, the car instinctively felt right. He won.

So enamored was Stewart that when he crashed the 003 in a non-championship race at Silverstone—the throttle had stuck open—he insisted that the team repair it for the next Grand Prix rather than using the 004. By the time the Tyrrells finished one-two at the French GP, other teams were muttering darkly that Tyrrell was cheating—that Stewart and Cevert had illegal fuel, or modified engines, or both. The organizers stripped both cars and found nothing amiss.

Stewart and the 003 were unstoppable—charmed, almost. When its oil scavenge pump broke 15 minutes before the start of the British GP, his mechanics intuitively cobbled together a fix with seconds to spare. He had the championship in his pocket by round eight of eleven, even though he failed to finish that race. In all, he won seven Grands Prix in the 003, six of them in 1971.

But Stewart's hectic work schedule—personal appearances, non-championship F1 races and entries in other series—was taking its toll on his health. He won the opening round of the 1972 season in the 003, but began to experience blurred vision and dizziness. At the next race, he tried the new 004 in practice but raced the 003. Its gearbox failed. To Stewart it seemed as if the 003 was becoming enfeebled too.

After finishing fourth at Monaco, spinning twice, Stewart sought medical advice and was diagnosed with a duodenal ulcer. Rather than have an operation and sit out races, he took medication and plowed on, winning the French GP on grit alone. But the Lotus 72 of Emerson Fittipaldi was proving almost unbeatable, and Tyrrell and Stewart reluctantly concluded that the 003's time as a competitive force was coming to an end.

At the German GP, the 003 lost its rear brakes and Stewart had a heavy accident with Clay Regazzoni, almost destroying the nose section. The damage was repairable—but the 003 would never take part in another Grand Prix. A remarkable story had reached its natural conclusion. By 1973 Stewart's own narrative was about to reach a new chapter; having weathered the deaths of so many friends during his racing career, he had already decided to retire when Cevert, in many ways his protégé, died in a crash at Watkins Glen.

Ah, Del Boy Gardner. Never made terribly pretty cars, but they were very functional. You had designers who were innovators and you had ones that were just good engineers—people who identified the best bits of what everyone else was doing. Derek was one of the latter. He could make a solid car, picking up the best points from other people.

Gordon Murray

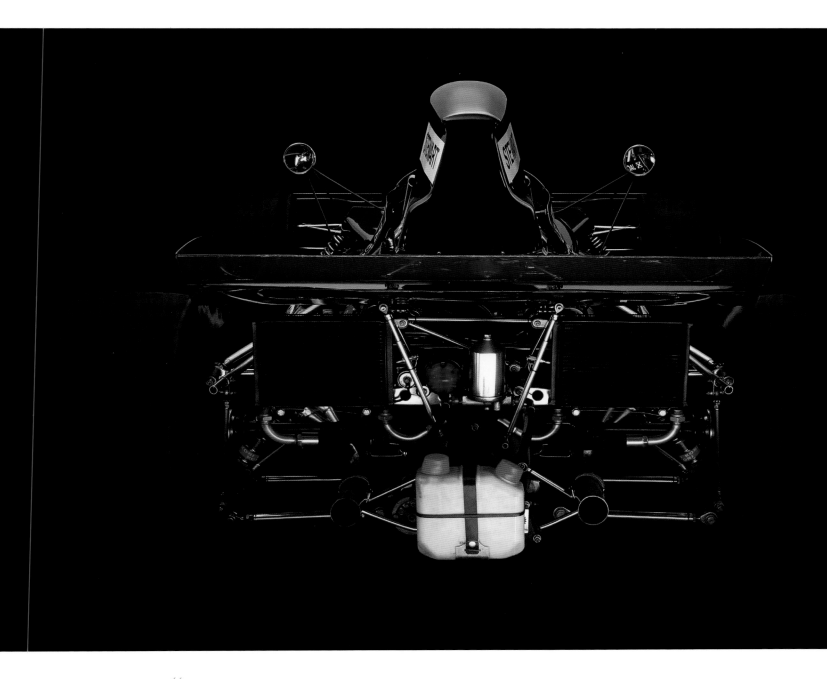

Monocoques were a step forward from space frames, and each year we got stiffer and stiffer on spring and damping rates. But the torsional rigidity wasn't keeping up with the extra input on the chassis. So if you built a car that had a big step forward in torsional rigidity, the car felt a hell of a lot more predictable and stable on the limit.

Gordon Murray

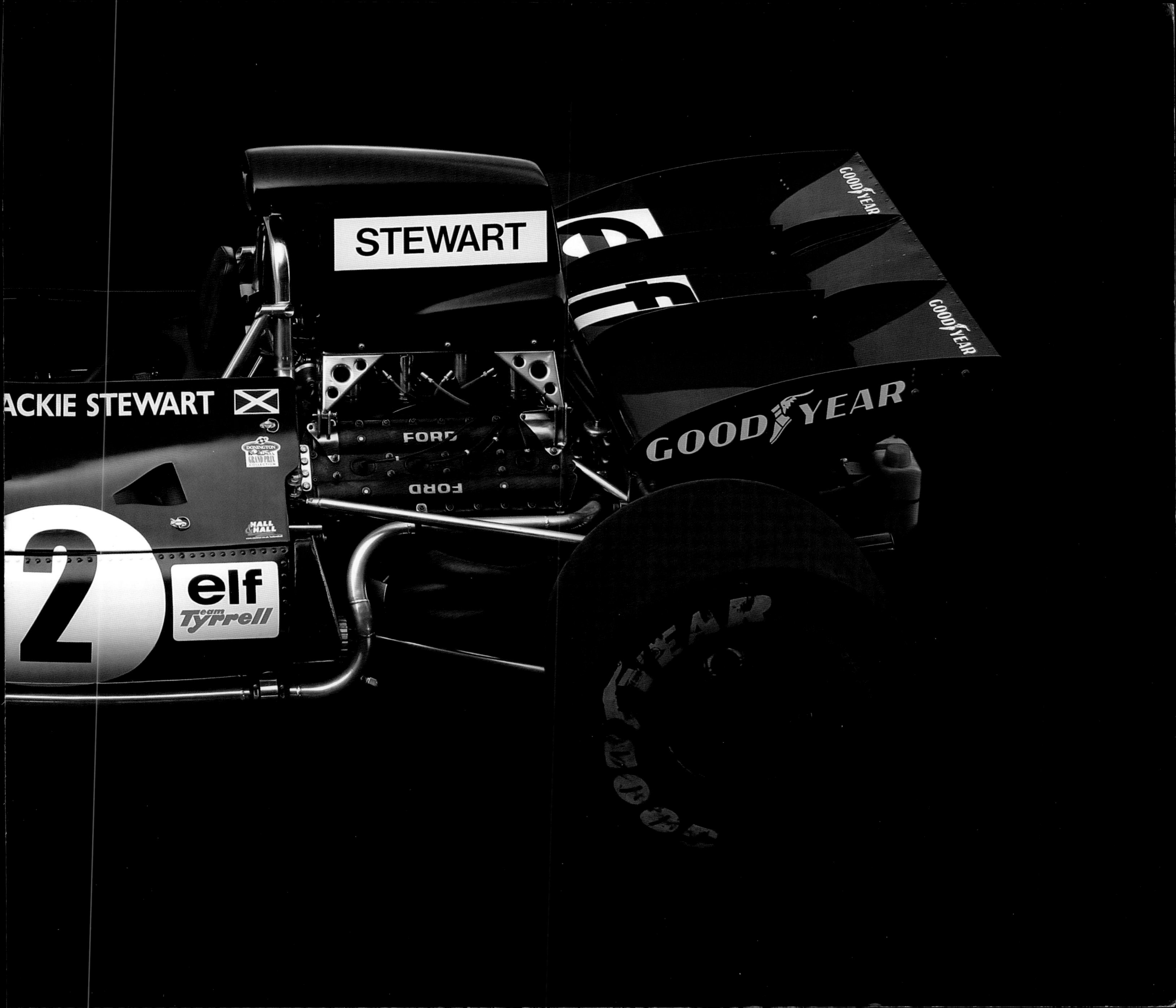
STEWART
ACKIE STEWART
FORD
FORD
GOODYEAR
GOODYEAR
GOODYEAR
2
elf
Team Tyrrell

> *Just looking at the spacing of the rivets on the 003, you can tell it was a very stiff car. Derek might have got a bit from the Matras. They came from the aerospace industry, so their cars were built like brick shithouses. And the 003 didn't have rocker-arm suspension; it had proper springs. No wonder Stewart liked it so much. He would probably have hated the Lotus 72—it would have been moving all over the place. He was such a fantastically precise driver; he would have wanted a car that was planted.*
>
> *Gordon Murray*

Tyrrell 003

First championship GP
Spain (Montjuich Park), 1971

Last championship GP
Germany (Nürburgring) 1972

Wins/championship races entered
8/16

Wins

Spain (Montjuich Park)	1971	Stewart
Monaco (Monte Carlo)	1971	Stewart
France (Paul Ricard)	1971	Stewart
Great Britain (Silverstone)	1971	Stewart
Germany (Nürburgring)	1971	Stewart
Canada (Mosport)	1971	Stewart
Argentina (Buenos Aires)	1972	Stewart
France (Clermont-Ferrand)	1972	Stewart

Engine
2,993-cc Ford-Cosworth V-8, 440 horsepower (est.)

10

Tyrrell P34

TO PRODUCE ONE CAR IN TOTAL SECRET takes guile and determination. To do it again, several years and two drivers' championships later, requires both those qualities and more—most notably that of loyalty. No one involved in the design and manufacture of the revolutionary six-wheeled "Project 34" breathed a word to the press; when Tyrrell unveiled it in September 1975, the reaction was stunned silence.

Nick Brittan, author of the irreverent "Private Ear" column in *Autosport*, described the scene:

"The expression that will remain etched on my mind for a long time was that of Frank Williams. Pure, honest, unadulterated, total disbelief. Eyes glazed. Jaw hanging open."

In the 1960s, before he joined Tyrrell, designer Derek Gardner had worked on a four-wheel-drive, gas turbine Indy car. The science of aerodynamics as applied to racing cars was still in its infancy, but engineers were well aware that the car's wheels were a major hurdle to straight-line speed—they obstructed the airflow and created turbulence.

Smaller wheels would be less of an impedance, but that would mean less rubber in contact with the road, reducing grip and cornering performance. Gardner briefly entertained the notion of creating a car with four smaller wheels up front instead of two large ones, but the Indy car project was canceled and he moved on to other projects.

www.historicracing.com

September 1975. Ken Tyrrell (second from right) presents Project 34 to the public. A bemused Frank Williams can be seen second from left. LAT Photographic

Having delivered the P34's first and only pole position the day before, Jody Scheckter muscles the car to its lone victory at the 1976 Swedish Grand Prix at Anderstorp. LAT Photographic

By the mid-1970s, Gardner felt the time was right to dust off his idea and try again. In 1973, Tyrrell had suffered the dual blow of François Cevert's death and Jackie Stewart's retirement; since then, the team hadn't enjoyed the same level of success, in spite of running the talented duo of Jody Scheckter and Patrick Depailler. Gardner felt that to win in an environment where most other teams ran the same engine, gearbox, and tires he would have to make a quantum leap in performance.

At the launch, Gardner said that winter testing—back to back against Tyrrell's existing cars—would prove decisively whether Project 34 was worth developing as a race car. But this was hardly a challenging benchmark since Tyrrell had been racing the same 007 chassis for the best part of two years.

The P34's theoretical advantage lay not in reduced frontal area—the rear wheels were no smaller than before—but in reduced lift from the front wheels. Combined with a low-slung chassis, which the driver seemed to sit on rather than in (early models had windows in the cockpit sides to help the drivers position the car in corners), and a narrow-track front, the new Tyrrell promised to be slippery and aero-balanced.

Predictably, the P34 blew off its antiquated forebears in testing. But it was not without problems: It was heavy, owing to the extra suspension componentry up front, and its brakes were excruciatingly difficult to balance. Depending on which of its front tires locked first, the P34's effective wheelbase (and therefore its handling) could change substantially. Scheckter disliked the car from his first acquaintance with it.

Tyrrell persisted with the 007 until the Spanish Grand Prix, the fourth race of the 1976 season. It was time for the new car to prove itself against its competitors; Depailler qualified third in the P34, 11 places ahead of Scheckter in the 007. But in the race, Depailler was dogged by brake problems and he spun out.

Over the following races, the P34 began to defy its critics. Scheckter drove one at the next GP, at Spa-Francorchamps, and finished fourth. Then he and Depailler finished on the podium at Monaco. It was clear that the P34, though heavy, generated excellent cornering "bite" from its four front wheels. At the next race, an otherwise drearily processional affair at Anderstorp in Sweden, Tyrrell went one better: Scheckter and Depailler inherited the one-two after Mario Andretti's engine failed. The car that so many experts had airily dismissed as an eccentric publicity stunt (if so, it had been successful in that field, too) had won a Grand Prix.

But it would never win another. Scheckter and Depailler claimed six more podiums and finished third and fourth in the drivers' championship, but the P34 was afflicted with a number of confidence-sapping reliability problems. The brakes would overheat, steering arms would break, and vital suspension components would fail. Scheckter was lying fourth in the Austrian GP, chasing the leading pack into the 160-mile-per-hour right-hander where Mark Donohue had lost his life the previous year, when his suspension gave way and pitched him sharply into the guardrail. He was lucky to survive with just a cut to his leg. Depailler was even luckier, for when his car suffered an identical failure it had less violent consequences.

Scheckter left the team at the end of the year and was replaced by Ronnie Peterson. Gardner produced a "B" version of the P34 for 1977 (pictured here) with a longer wheelbase and wider front track. The driver sat significantly lower in the cockpit, and the all-new bodywork had a less sheer and altogether more elegant profile. Tyrrell also landed a new sponsor, the First National City bank.

The 1977 season was demoralizingly poor. The P34B regularly overheated—the oil coolers weren't getting enough air—and its handling grew ever more imbalanced as Goodyear continued to develop new compounds for conventional rims but allowed the 10-inch size to lie fallow. Its front brakes often cooked, and its one-piece bodywork was cumbersome to transport to races. The team scored just four podium finishes; Niki Lauda won the drivers' title for Ferrari, but the resurgent Lotus team was demonstrating the virtues of "ground-effect" aerodynamics with its brisk but unreliable 78. The six-wheeler looked like an evolutionary dead end in comparison.

Gardner quit before the Italian GP and would never design another F1 car. Scheckter felt vindicated. "It was a rubbish car," he said.

The P34 story has a fascinating postscript. In 1997, Simon Bull, a British TV presenter and expert on antique timepieces, got together with Gardner and historic racer Martin Stretton to buy and run a P34B in the Thoroughbred Grand Prix series. The Avon tire company produced some bespoke new rubber for the car, and the P34B has been racing—and winning—ever since.

Would F1 history have read differently if Goodyear had developed the 10-inch tires? It is a fascinating possibility.

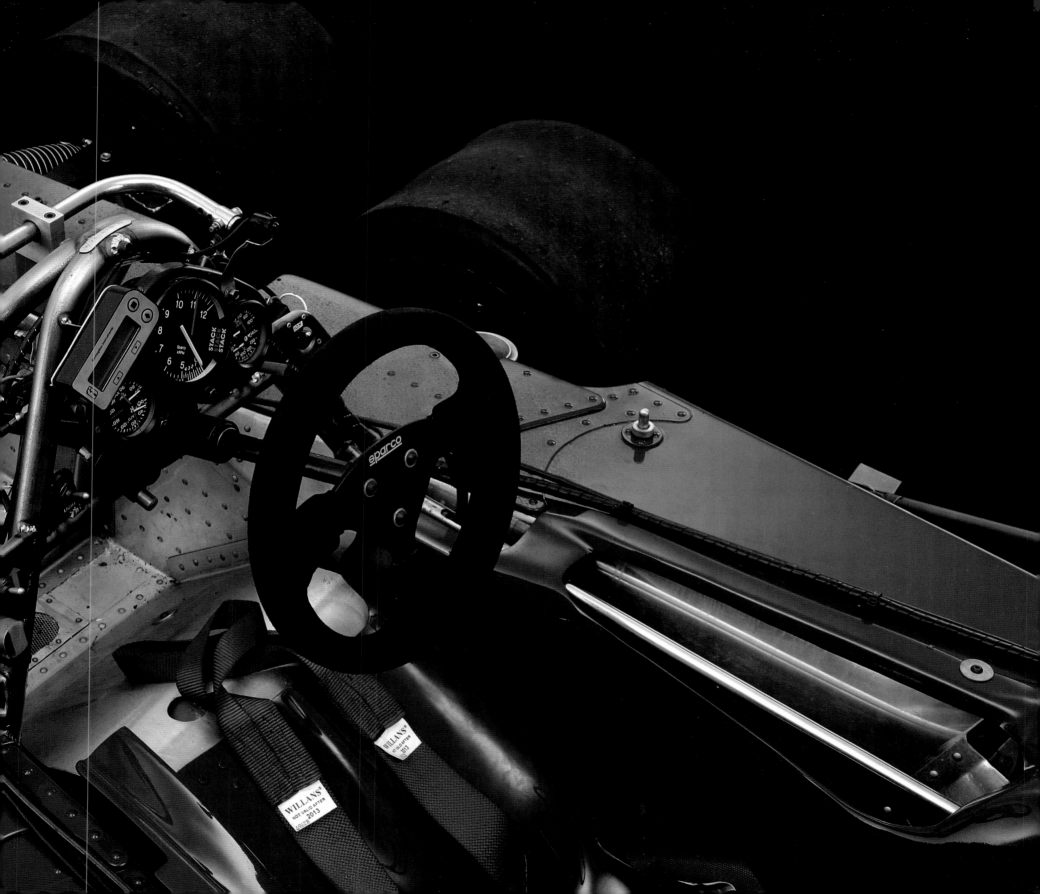

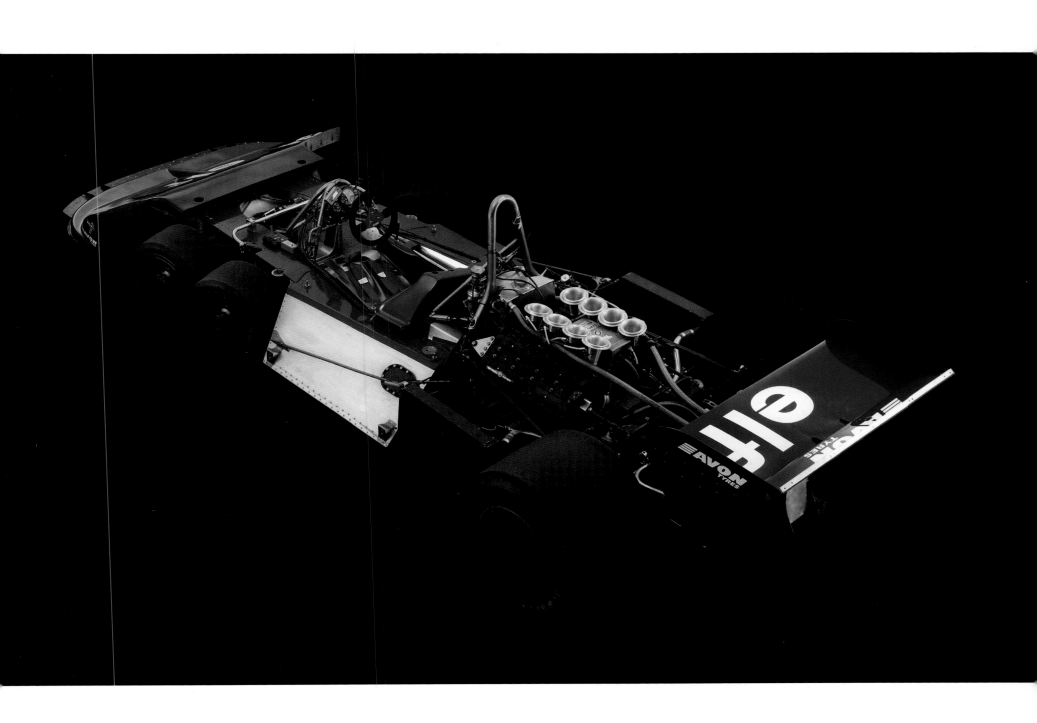

I never understood this car—never understood the reason for it. To reduce the frontal area, it would have been better to run four smaller rear wheels. As it is, the rear wheels are still sticking out and the frontal area hasn't decreased. But it would definitely have had less overall drag.

Countering that, it would have had a third more rolling resistance—and much more complexity. Not just static complexity, but reliability as well—lots more parts to break, and a third more chance of having a tire problem. And it would have been much more difficult to set up.

Sometimes, particularly with Chapman, someone would bring a new car out and you'd think, 'That's it—I've got to catch up now.' This was one of those cars that never worried me. I just didn't see the point. But it was very brave—and must have involved a hell of a lot of work.

Gordon Murray

Tyrrell P34

First championship GP
Spain (Jarama), 1976

Last championship GP
Japan (Fuji), 1977

Wins/championship races entered
1/30

Wins
Sweden (Anderstorp)   1976   Scheckter

Engine
2,993-cc Ford-Cosworth V-8, 480 horsepower (est.)

11

Ferrari 312T3

EVEN BEFORE THE ACCIDENT THAT scarred him for life, Niki Lauda's fights with Enzo Ferrari over money had become the stuff of legend. Lauda had helped drag the team out of a rut and delivered the drivers' championship in 1975; to his mind, he was merely asking for what he deserved. Every year, Ferrari would rail against Lauda's impertinence and then quietly pay up.

But that appalling, nearly fatal accident at the 1976 German Grand Prix was the beginning of the end of their relationship. Although Lauda returned to the cockpit just six weeks later, missing only one race, at the final GP of the year he declared the wet conditions at Fuji Speedway too dangerous. He withdrew, leaving James Hunt to only have to finish in fourth place or better to win the championship. Ferrari never forgave him. In late 1977, with four races left to run and Lauda holding a 21-point lead in the championship, the two met again to discuss terms. Ferrari asked Lauda how much he wished to be paid in 1978.

"Nothing," said Lauda. "I'm leaving."

He finished second in the Italian GP, enough to establish an unbeatable championship lead, and then never drove a Ferrari again. Ferrari replaced him with a young French-Canadian who had just been passed up by McLaren despite an impressive handful of showings: Gilles Villeneuve.

Before his departure, Lauda had declared his car, the 312T2, "useless and finished." His teammate, Carlos Reutemann, took a more pragmatic view:

One of the most electrifying drivers in Formula 1 history, Gilles Villeneuve would soon make the tifosi *forget Niki Lauda.*
LAT Photographic

A po-faced Carlos Reuteman walks away from the wreckage after the Ferrari 312T3's brief but spectacular debut at the 1978 South African Grand Prix at Kyalami. LAT Photographic

"We have a good engine, a good gearbox and good brakes, which is more than some teams have," he said. "We just can't get them all balanced together to make a complete car."

The 312T3 bore a family resemblance to its predecessors but was very different under the skin. The first 312T had been designed for the 1975 season by Mauro Forghieri, one of the few engineers ever to have fallen out of favor with Enzo Ferrari and then been called back. The "T" designated a transverse gearbox, for the philosophy of this design was to be compact and nicely balanced to make the most of the mighty flat-12 engine. It was good enough for Lauda to win the drivers' title in 1977. But Enzo remained unhappy with the tire situation, feeling that he wanted to work with a company that would give him exclusive attention. At the end of 1977, he terminated his contract with Goodyear and took up with Michelin, who was also supplying Renault—but Enzo didn't view those quirky new turbo cars as a threat.

The T3 wasn't ready for the first two races of the 1978 season, but Reutemann demonstrated the potential of Michelin's radials by putting his T2 on the front row at the Argentine GP. He and the team then chose the wrong tires for the race, but after pitting for a fresh set of a different compound, he charged from 15th place to 7th. And at the Brazilian GP, the T2's swansong, the team made no such error and Reutemann simply tore away from the field.

As well as having a completely new monocoque and revised aerodynamics (the product of research in the Pininfarina wind tunnel), the T3 had different suspension geometry to make the most of the new Michelins. Forghieri thoroughly redesigned the rear suspension, including the gearbox casing it mounted to. At the front, he changed from a rocker-arm design to tubular wishbones with long vertical spring units.

At the South African GP, the T3 failed to make a glittering debut; Villeneuve's engine expired, dropping oil that Reutemann then drove over and slid straight on, into the catch fencing. Chassis 34, photographed here, was the third T3 to be built and

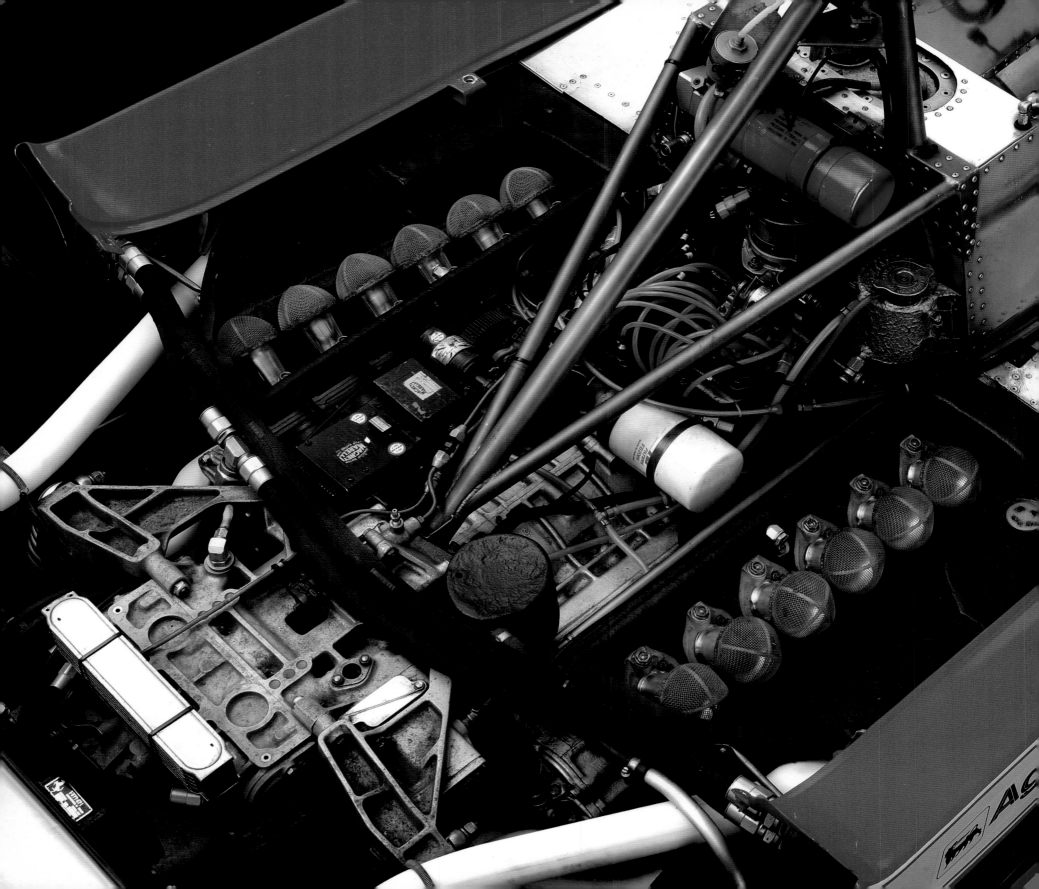

Gilles Villeneuve demonstrating his relentless driving style—total commitment, always on the limit, and often beyond. LAT Photographic

made its first appearance at Long Beach. Villeneuve qualified second and led the first half of the race until he crashed out while lapping Clay Regazzoni in the dawdling Shadow. Reutemann won.

Forghieri had a new rear wing ready for Monaco. Reutemann claimed pole position but fluffed the start and then tangled with Lauda. At race six, the Belgian GP at Zolder, Lotus unveiled its new 79. Although Reutemann started on the front row, he was almost a second slower than pole-sitter Mario Andretti—and once again, he didn't get away from the line cleanly, this time because he couldn't select second gear. Reutemann and Villeneuve finished third and fourth, a lap ahead of the cars behind them but well in arrears to the Lotuses of Andretti and Ronnie Peterson.

The season developed into a battle between the aerodynamically sophisticated but not always reliable Lotus and Ferrari's combination of flat-12 grunt and Michelin grip. When the tire choice was right, Ferrari was in with a shout. Mostly, though, it was outgunned by the 79's aerodynamics: The Lotus had venturi concealed in its sidepods that acted like upside-down aircraft wings, generating downforce that increased grip in corners. Lotus had moved the fuel tank behind the driver and redesigned the rear suspension to leave a clear path for the air through the sidepods. There was no easy way to redesign the T3 to mimic this because the Ferrari engine's horizontal cylinder heads were a potential obstacle for the airflow.

Reutemann, one of that subset of drivers who are only at their scintillating best when the car is perfect, made up his mind to leave for Lotus. Villeneuve just drove the wheels off the T3 whether he was fighting for first or tenth, and for that he was venerated by Enzo Ferrari and the legions of Ferrari fans.

Peterson's tragic death at Monza left Lotus in disarray, and Ferrari cleaned up at the last two races of the year. Villeneuve signed off the season with a win in chassis 34 at his home Grand Prix on Montreal's new Île Notre-Dame circuit. Although Forghieri produced another evolution of the 312T for 1979, featuring Lotus-like ground-effect aerodynamics, it was Villeneuve's new teammate, Jody Scheckter, who won the championship.

Villeneuve's spectacular driving style earned him the devotion of F1 fans worldwide, but he was destined never to win the drivers' title. Ferrari's persistence with the flat-12 engine led to a dramatic slump in form as other teams perfected ground effect. In 1982, having switched to turbocharged engines, Ferrari at last provided Villeneuve with a race-winning car once again; but he died in a shocking accident in qualifying for the Dutch GP. He left an indelible, inspiring legend—and one that would forever be associated with Ferrari.

So they were playing catch-up on chassis technology—but for the period, it was beautifully clean, aerodynamically. And the powertrain, of course, was a Ferrari strong-point. If you had a 12-cylinder engine that worked well in the late 1970s, you were quids in.

Gordon Murray

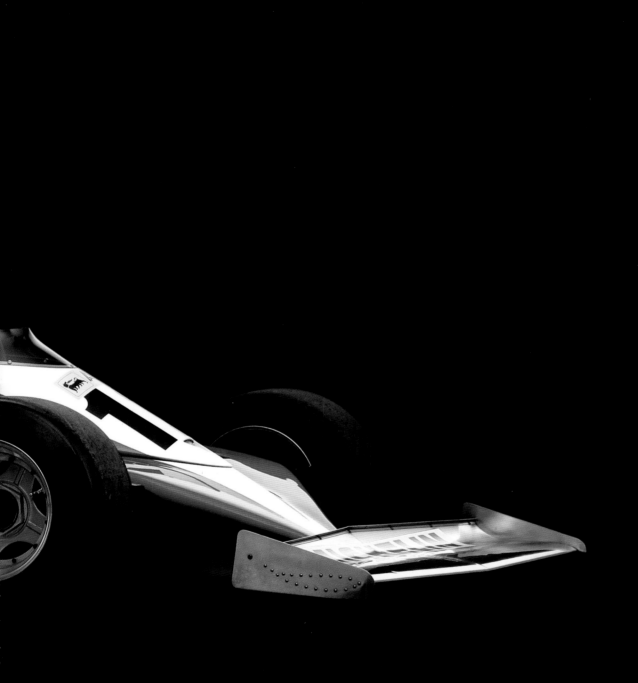

The biggest advantage this car had was the very clean air to the front and rear wings. If you look at the other cars of the era, they were stuffing radiators under the wing, and lumps and bumps and stuff. This is much more like the modern Formula 1 cars, where the front wing is an entity in itself and the bodywork behind it interferes very little. There's a very smooth lead-up to the rear wing from the deck of the car. The idea of the full-length sidepod was also clever and elegant.

Gordon Murray

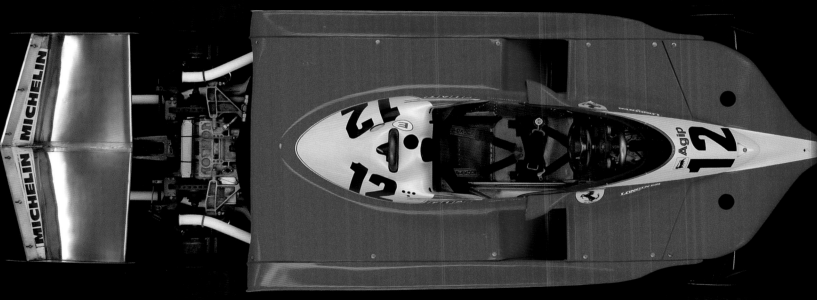

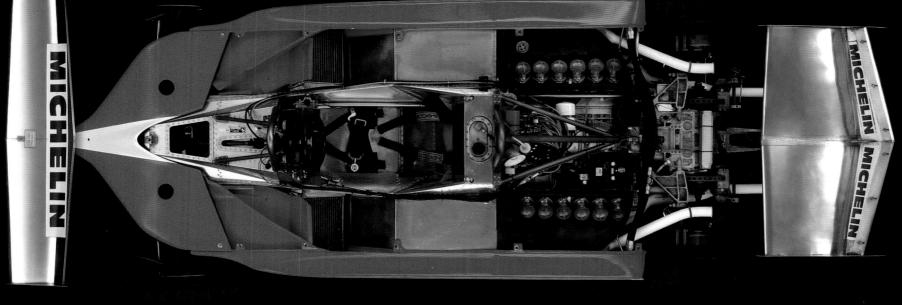

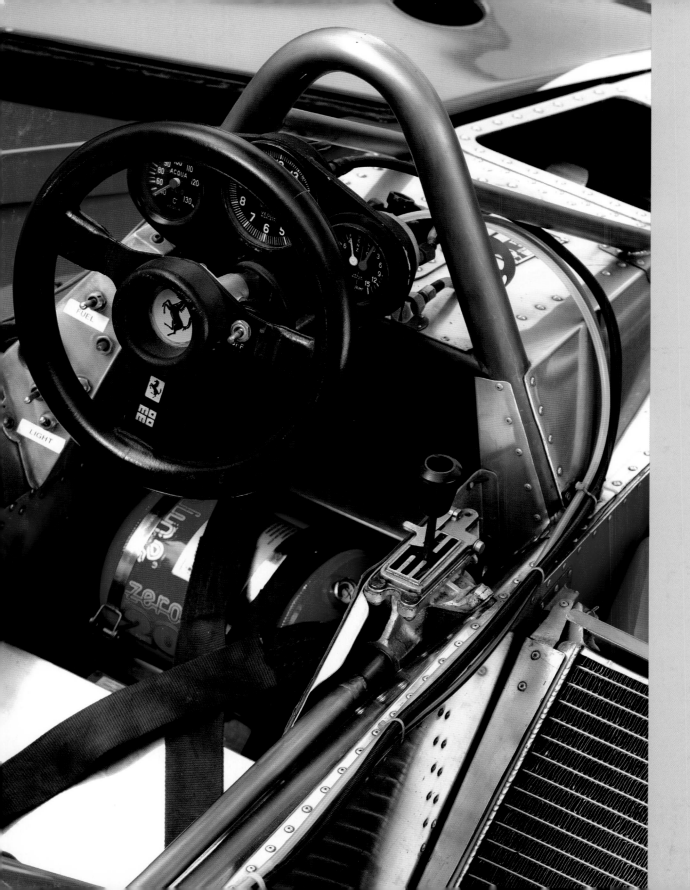

At the time—and it's nothing to do with Mauro, he's a good friend of mine—Ferrari was suffering enormously from trying to understand and catch up on monocoque technology. Their monocoques were really messy, very floppy, and not very strong at all. They were largely bunches of lightweight tubes with aluminum pop-riveted to them. If you saw one of these Ferraris with the body off, they were quite messy—and nowhere near as torsionally stiff as the British cars.

Gordon Murray

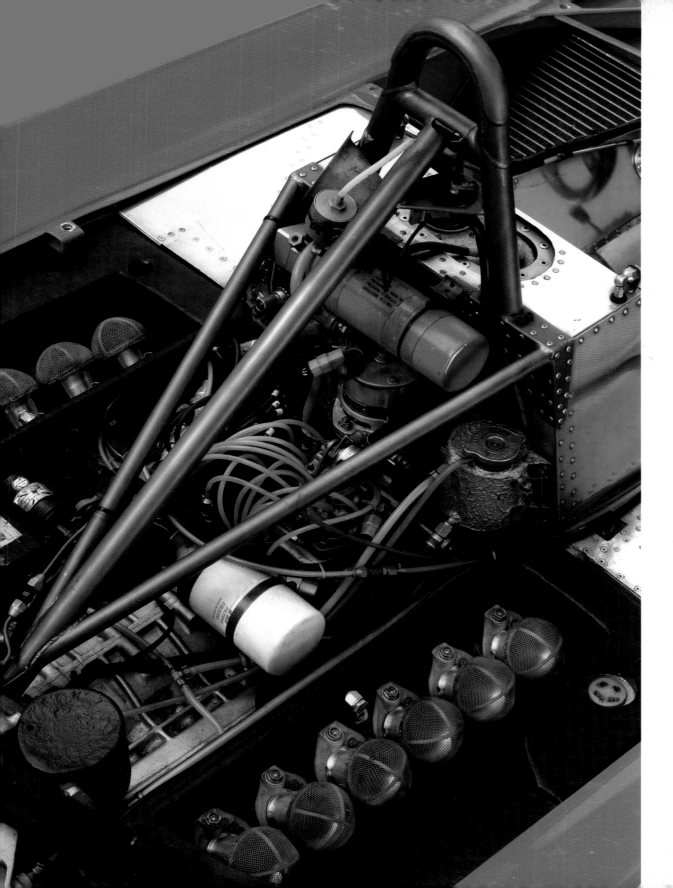

Ferrari 312T3

First championship GP
South Africa (Kyalami), 1978

Last championship GP
Brazil (Interlagos) 1979

Wins/championship races entered
4/16

Wins
U.S. (Long Beach)	1978	Reutemann
Great Britain (Brands Hatch)	1978	Reutemann
U.S. (Watkins Glen)	1978	Reutemann
Canada (Montreal)	1978	Villeneuve

Engine
2,991-cc Ferrari flat-12, 510 horsepower (est.)

12
Williams FW07

FRANK WILLIAMS WAS THE SORT OF BOY who would hitchhike all over the country to visit motor races, with all the personal risks that entailed. Is it any surprise that he should have grown up to lead one of the most successful Formula 1 teams of all-time?

Success didn't come easily. In the early years, he plowed all his earnings as a traveling salesman into paying for race drives. Then he quit that job to work as a mechanic in Formula Junior. Even after establishing Frank Williams Racing Cars in 1967, running his friend Piers Courage in an old Brabham F1 car, he still had to do deals from public call boxes and for lack of funds was derided in the F1 paddock as "Wanker Williams."

During the 1970s Frank's team lived from hand to mouth. After losing control of the team to his partner, oil magnate Walter Wolf, he set up again as Williams Grand Prix Engineering in 1977, running Belgian pay-driver Patrick Neve in a year-old March 761. But behind the scenes, he was planning a racing renaissance with the FW06, a car designed by Patrick Head, the talented engineer who was now Williams' business partner.

Through personal connections, Williams acquired Saudia sponsorship, giving him enough finance to employ a proper driver. He chose Alan Jones, a gritty Australian who epitomized everything that Frank and Patrick desired in a racer. Jones was ballsy, no-nonsense, and quick. He finished in the

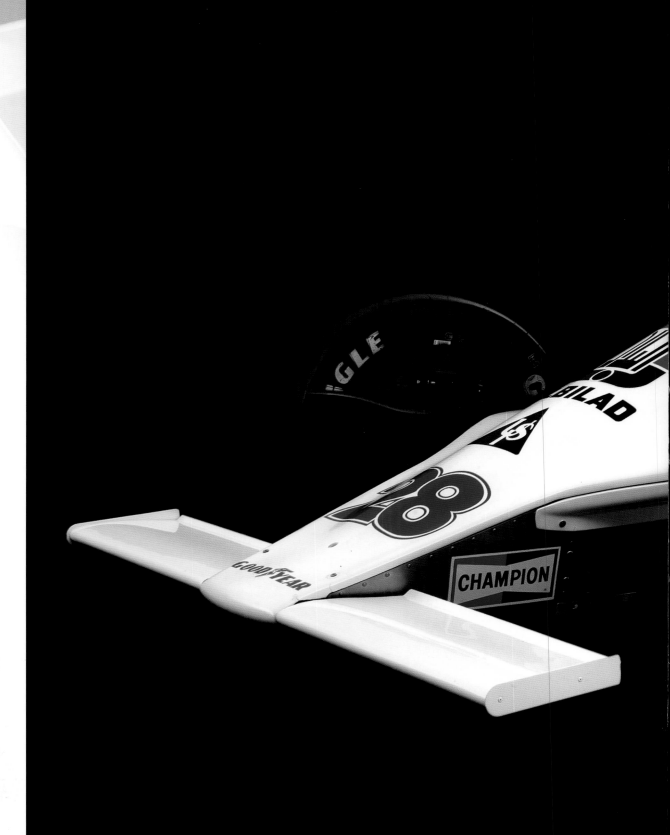

Patrick Head (left) and Frank Williams at the new Williams factory in Didcot, Oxfordshire, England, in 1978. *Williams F1 Team*

Alan Jones: The prototypical Williams driver. *Williams F1 Team*

points three times in 1978—including a podium at Watkins Glen—but although the FW06 was neat and effective, it was outclassed by the new generation of ground-effect cars led by the Lotus 79.

Lotus had been careful to guard the secrets of the 79's speed, even concealing its differential under a tea cosy to lure rivals into believing that a trick diff was the key. The real secret was an array of inverted air foils concealed in the sidepods, which created a low-pressure area under the car, increasing cornering grip. In November 1979, Head and his colleagues went into the Donald Campbell wind tunnel at Imperial College with a scale model (25 percent was the largest the tunnel could accommodate) resembling the 79 to decode its tricks.

For "ground effect" to work at its optimum, the underside of the car had to be sealed at the sides. Lotus had discovered this by accident, when a model made from balsawood and tape sagged in the wind tunnel. Through experimentation, Head learned that a small front wing made the sidepods work more effectively; thus, he designed the FW07 with a minimal wing and much longer sidepods. Another Williams engineer, Frank Dernie, devised a highly efficient skirting system (more effective, they believed, than the 79's) to seal the underfloor.

Where the 79 had inboard rear disc brakes—a typical Lotus feature designed to reduce unsprung weight—Head located them outboard on the FW07. He saw a greater benefit in having a more spacious exit route for the air—and in having brakes that worked more effectively. The team expanded to a two-car operation for 1979, recruiting the Swiss veteran Clay Regazzoni to join Jones, but the FW07 wasn't ready until the fifth race of the season.

On its debut at Jarama, the FW07 proved more competitive in the race than in qualifying, but both drivers retired with mechanical failure. Jones qualified fourth for the next race, the Belgian GP at Zolder, and led until an electrical failure ruled him out. At Monaco, Regazzoni finished second overall after charging through the field from sixteenth on

the grid. Soon, the team's pleasure at having designed a competitive car began to slide into frustration at not having won a Grand Prix with it.

Williams didn't have to wait long. At Silverstone, his team's home GP, Head modified the cars with aluminum panels to join the rear wing to the floor, sealing off the airflow around the engine. Jones claimed pole position with a lap almost two seconds quicker than the next fastest cars, the Renaults of René Arnoux and Jean-Pierre Jabouille. But it wasn't to be Jones' race: The housing of his water pump, which had been modified to accommodate the new bodywork, cracked while he was leading on lap 38. Regazzoni's pump held up, and he won by 25 seconds from Arnoux. Everyone else was a lap behind. After ten years of scratching about at the margins, Frank Williams had finally laid his nickname to rest.

Jones won four of the six remaining Grands Prix and finished third in the drivers' standings, 11 points

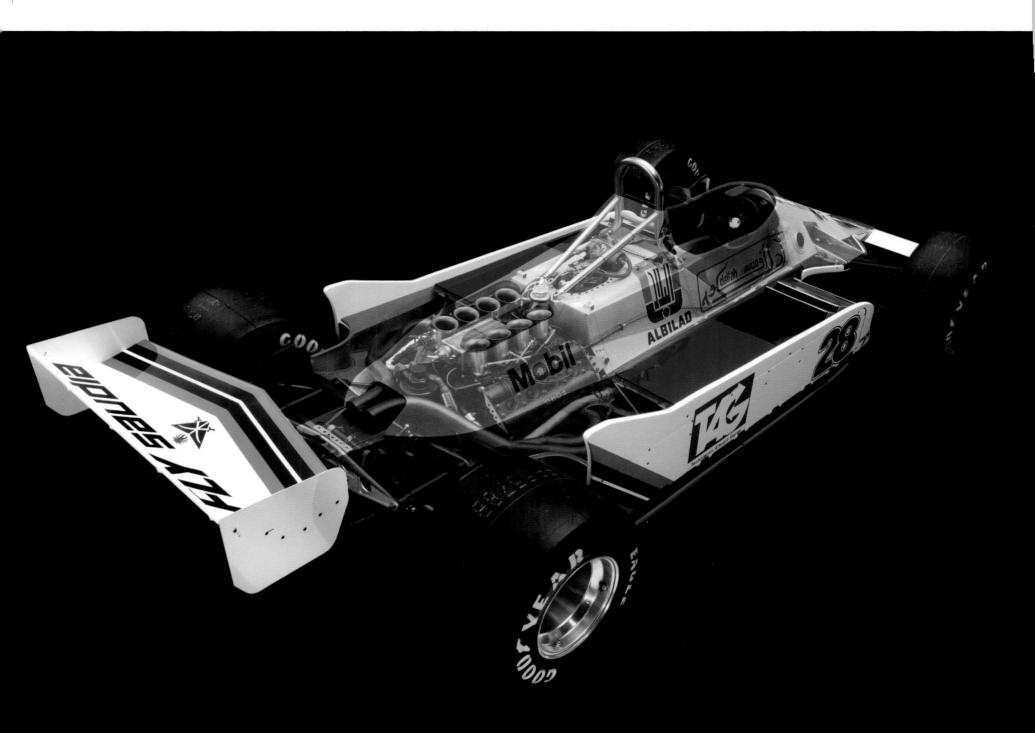

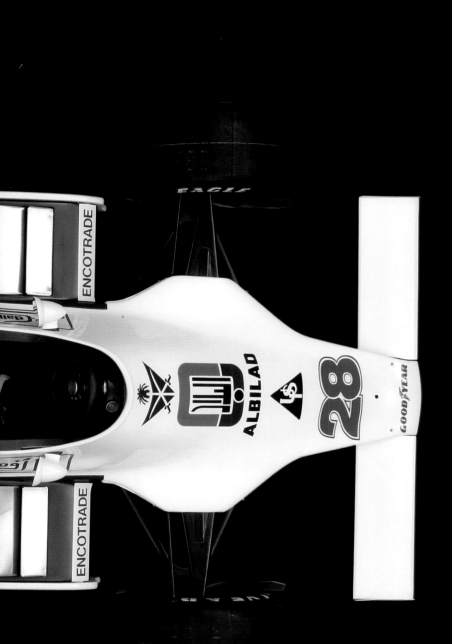

short of champion Jody Scheckter. Regazzoni was fifth overall, but Williams felt he qualified poorly and took too long to wake up to race pace. In any case, Regazzoni was 40 years old, so Williams replaced him with Carlos Reutemann for 1980.

Head developed a "B" spec of the FW07, strengthening the suspension and doing away with the front wing entirely. Famously, the relationship between Jones and Reutemann curdled into outright acrimony, but it didn't stop Jones from winning five Grands Prix and the drivers' title that year.

Reutemann should have won the 1981 championship, but he lost fourth gear in the final race of the year, on a temporary course in the parking lot of the Caesars Palace casino in Las Vegas, and faded away to eighth place. Brabham's Nelson Piquet finished fifth, snatching the drivers' title, although Williams had enough points to win the constructors' championship for a second consecutive year. In "D" spec the FW07 raced in the first three GPs of 1982, until the FW08 was ready; Keke Rosberg took the FW07 to a podium finish at Long Beach, its final outing, although Mario Andretti (making a one-off appearance for the team) failed to finish.

Many of those involved in the design of the FW07 went on to achieve long-term success in F1. Draftsman Neil Oatley became McLaren's chief designer, working on championship winners spanning over two decades. Dernie honed Michael Schumacher into a champion at Benetton. Ross Brawn machined many of the FW07's components before training as an aerodynamicist, and in later years was technical director of Benetton and Ferrari at the height of their powers.

Between 1980 and 1997, Williams won the constructors' championship nine times, seldom innovating, but always taking the best technology available—and improving it. As Head was once heard to growl down the radio to his driver, Antonio Pizzonia, during one of the team's low points in 2004: "Whatever it is that you do—do it better!"

Regazzoni on his way to delivering the Williams team's first Formula 1 victory at the 1979 British Grand Prix at Silverstone. Williams F1 Team

Reutemann at the 1981 U.S. Grand Prix in the Williams FW07C. After qualifying on pole, the championship appeared to be his for the taking, but the enigmatic Argentine would go on to finish a pointless eighth. Williams F1 Team

"*Patrick Head is another one of those solid engineers. He was excellent at looking around at what everyone else was doing and then making a better version of it. This whole period of Williams chassis was like that—not innovating in their own right, but really making the best of what was around and turning it into a solidly engineered car that could win a championship.*"

Gordon Murray

Williams FW07

First championship GP
Spain (Jarama), 1979

Last championship GP
U.S. (Long Beach), 1982

Wins/championship races entered
15/43

Wins

Britain (Silverstone)	1979	Regazzoni
Germany (Hockenheim)	1979	Jones
Austria (Österreichring)	1979	Jones
Netherlands (Zandvoort)	1979	Jones
Canada (Montreal)	1979	Jones
Argentina (Buenos Aires)	1980	Jones
Monaco (Monte Carlo)	1980	Reutemann
France (Paul Ricard)	1980	Jones
Britain (Brands Hatch)	1980	Jones
Canada (Montreal)	1980	Jones
U.S. (Watkins Glen)	1980	Jones
U.S. (Long Beach)	1981	Jones
Brazil (Rio de Janeiro)	1981	Reutemann
Belgium (Zolder)	1981	Reutemann
U.S. (Las Vegas)	1981	Jones

Engine
2,993-cc Ford-Cosworth V-8, 490 horsepower (est.)

13
McLaren MP4/4

TO SAY THAT THE McLAREN MP4/4 dominated the 1988 Formula 1 season is an enormous understatement: Not only did it win 15 out of the 16 races, earning almost as many points as the rest of the field put together, but it led for all but 28 racing laps. The team's gradual decline in competitiveness over the preceding seasons had slammed abruptly into reverse.

John Barnard, who had led the design team with almost dictatorial perfectionism since 1980 and revolutionized F1 engineering with the first fully carbon-fiber chassis, had left McLaren in August 1986. At the time, Alain Prost, driving Barnard's TAG/Porsche-powered McLaren MP4/2C, was embroiled in a fierce championship battle with the Williams-Hondas of Nigel Mansell and Nelson Piquet—Prost would clinch his second drivers' title at the final round of the year, but only after Mansell's rear tires exploded and Williams brought Piquet in for a precautionary pit stop. Temporarily rudderless, the design team hurried through the evolutionary MP4/3; Prost won three Grands Prix with it in 1987, but it was thoroughly outclassed by the Williams-Honda. Everything was to change in 1988, though.

McLaren signed the gifted Ayrton Senna from Lotus, technical director Gordon Murray from Brabham, and secured a supply of Honda's mighty V-6 turbo engines. The new car was to be just that— all new. Until then, every successive member of the

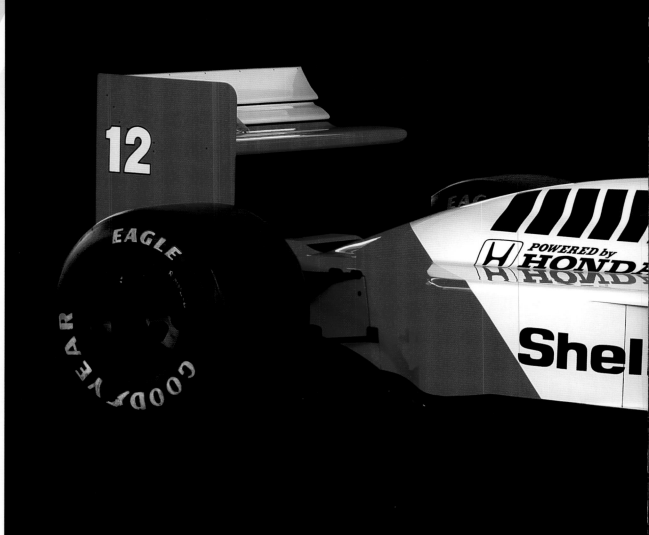

Detroit arrived on the F1 scene as host for the U.S. Grand Prix in 1982, but most drivers disliked the dull layout and slippery surface. Senna won from pole position in the last GP to be held here, in 1988. LAT Photographic

Alain Prost cruised serenely to victory after Ayrton Senna started the Spanish GP at Jerez from pole position but had to back off when his on-board computer told him to economize on fuel. LAT Photographic

MP4 family had been built around an evolution of the first MP4's revolutionary carbon-fiber monocoque; but it had been built with ground-effect aerodynamics in mind, with a narrow base to leave plenty of space on either side for venturi in the sidepods. By 1987, this design merely yielded a car with an unnecessarily high center of gravity and a somewhat-bloated aero profile.

The MP4/4 was a clean-sheet design from the monocoque up, sharing many themes with Murray's daring but unsuccessful "skateboard" Brabham BT55. Its wheelbase was 40 millimeters longer than the MP4/3's, and the Honda engine could be mounted usefully lower, benefiting both the aerodynamics and the handling. The driving position was aggressively reclined, too.

In an attempt to equalize performance, the FIA announced that turbo engines would be outlawed in 1989 and for the 1988 season would be subject to strict performance limits: a reduction in boost pressures and fuel tank capacities. But Honda was determined to end the turbo era on top and produced an entirely new engine—lighter, more compact, and well suited to the design priorities of the MP4/4.

Finished so late that it only undertook one day of testing before the start of the season, the MP4/4 nevertheless blitzed every Grand Prix of the year. It was helped by the weakness of the opposition: Williams had lost the Honda contract, and Lotus, which had held on to the Honda supply, was so far behind that the team was reduced to griping that McLaren was cheating. After the Canadian Grand Prix, the FIA stripped both MP4/4s down, convinced that McLaren had somehow circumvented the fuel limit. The FIA found nothing amiss. The first non-McLaren to lead a lap was Gerhard Berger's Ferrari—during the eighth race of the year.

Behind the scenes, all was not well. Having safely outpaced his previous teammates, Prost was thoroughly discombobulated by the arrival of the intense and ambitious Senna. Both felt entitled

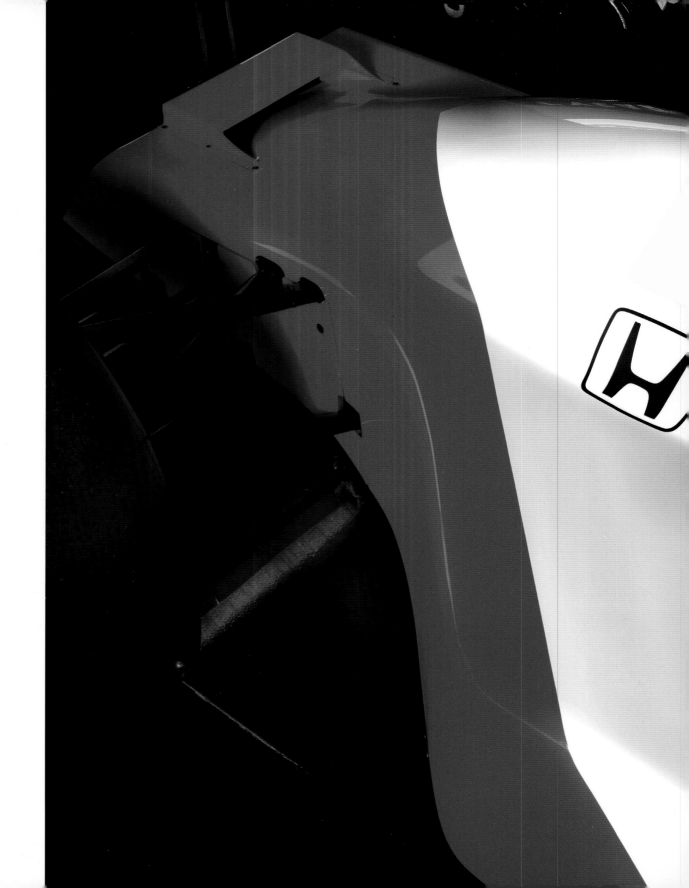

to undisputed number-one status; their fractious relationship eventually boiled over into outright rancor and became one of the sport's greatest-ever rivalries. They would partner again in the 1989 season, but by then were not on speaking terms, and the 1989 championship fell to Prost after he and Senna collided in the Japanese GP.

It is difficult to quantify the MP4/4's margin of superiority because it was conducted by two of the greatest drivers of the age. The turbo restrictions gave the atmospheric engines a theoretical advantage; but because either Prost or Senna—or both—was driving at the absolute limit at any given time, the MP4/4 always fulfilled its maximum potential. The one race it failed to win suggests how slim its advantage may have been: Holding a substantial lead in the closing laps of the Italian GP, Senna came up to lap Jean-Louis Schlesser's dawdling Williams and made a seemingly impulsive dive up the inside. Schlesser failed to see Senna coming, turned in to the corner, and eliminated them both. Gerhard Berger gladly inherited a memorable home victory for Ferrari less than a month after Enzo Ferrari's death.

But Senna had *needed* to hustle. The McLaren team had blown an engine in practice, and Honda had enriched the fuel mixture to prevent it happening again. In those final laps, Senna was running critically low on fuel, and just to get to the end he had to maximize his corner speed at every opportunity. Backing off to attack Schlesser later in the lap could have left him without enough fuel to finish the race; thus, he made the split-second decision to pass where he did. This, then, was the one that got away.

Declaring himself fed up with Formula 1's increasingly prescriptive technical regulations, Murray departed at the end of 1988 to head up McLaren's road car project. The F1 design team, led by Neil Oatley, carried on producing championship-winning cars: It was 1992 before McLaren could be toppled again.

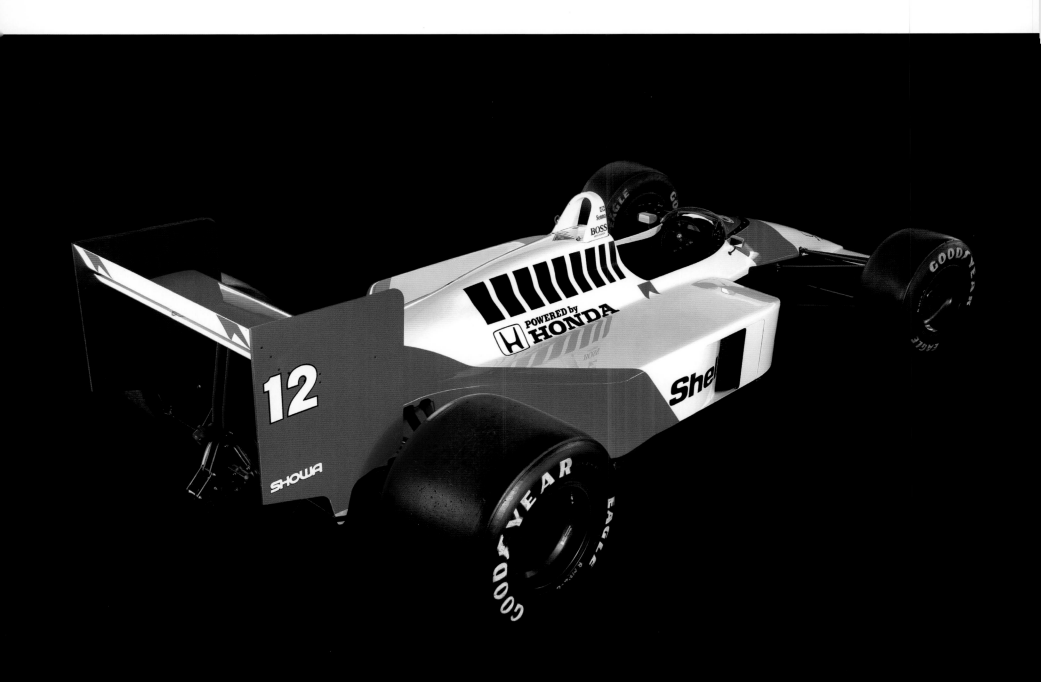

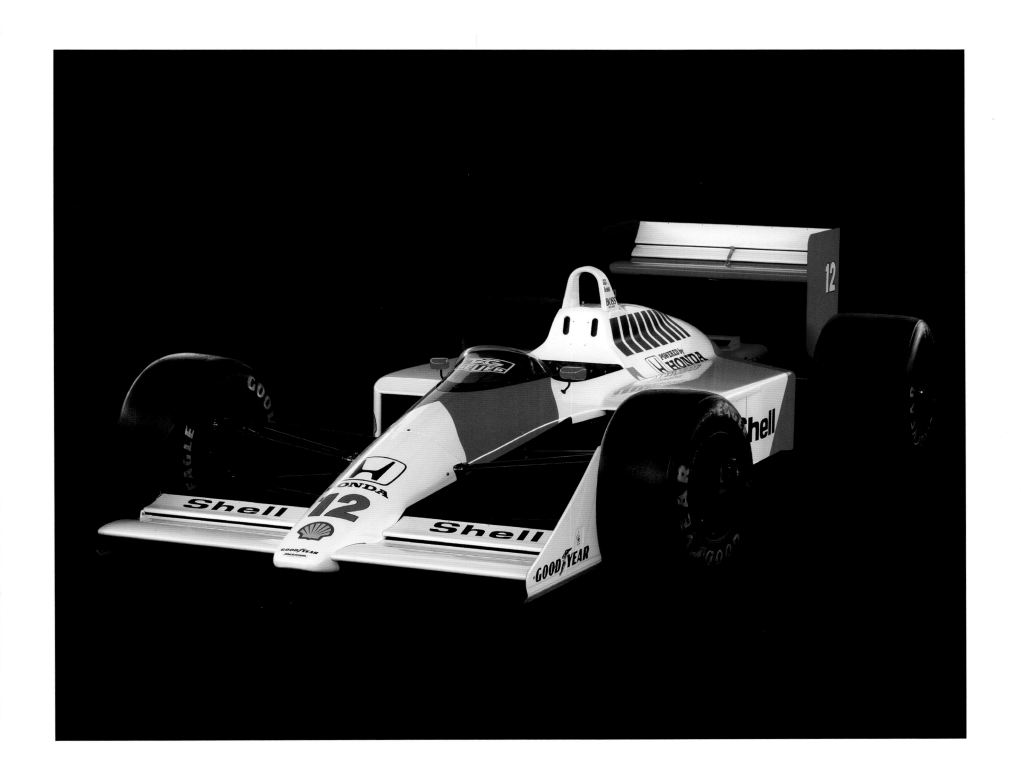

"It was such a simple car, but we found a massive improvement in the aerodynamics. And it handled very well.

I've always loved very simple things. I wanted to bring the driver back down to Chapman levels. Over the years, they'd been creeping back up again; the designers were looking to package more and more fuel behind the driver, and the engines were getting bigger, so the cam covers and trumpets were getting higher and higher. There was no point in having the driver low—until we got to the turbo era.

Honda was able to lower the crank line of the V-6—it was tiny anyway. We did a special three-shaft gearbox to bring the drive up to the right level."

Gordon Murray

McLaren MP4/4

First championship GP
Brazil (Jacarepaguá), 1988

Last championship GP
Australia (Adelaide), 1988

Wins/championship races entered
15/16

Wins

Brazil (Jacarepaguá)	1988	Prost
San Marino (Imola)	1988	Senna
Monaco (Monte Carlo)	1988	Prost
Mexico (Mexico City)	1988	Prost
Canada (Montreal),	1988	Senna
U.S. (Detroit)	1988	Senna
France (Paul Ricard)	1988	Prost
Britain (Silverstone)	1988	Senna
Germany (Hockenheim)	1988	Senna
Hungary (Hungaroring)	1988	Senna
Belgium (Spa-Francorchamps)	1988	Senna
Portugal (Estoril)	1988	Prost
Spain (Jerez)	1988	Prost
Japan (Suzuka)	1988	Senna
Australia (Adelaide)	1988	Prost

Engine
1,494-cc Honda V-6, turbocharged, 680 horsepower
(claimed)

Leyton House CG901

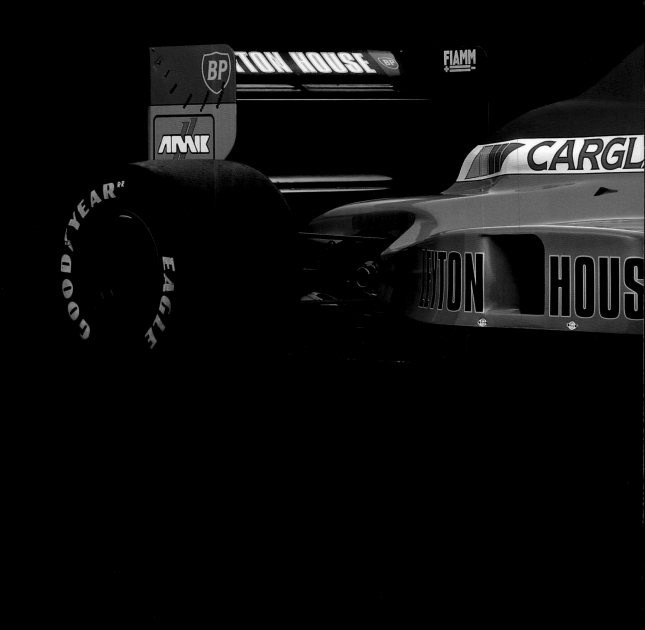

LEYTON HOUSE MAY NOT BE A NAME that carries profound resonance in the pantheon of Grand Prix racing, and yet on July 8, 1990, this tiny team came within three laps of causing one of the greatest upsets in Formula 1 history. Its young Italian driver, Ivan Capelli, led most of the French Grand Prix with the Ferrari of reigning-champion Alain Prost tucked under his rear wing. For a few brief moments, the hitherto unfancied CG901 appeared about to execute a quiet revolution in the world of F1 aerodynamics; and yet two weeks earlier, in Mexico, Capelli and teammate Mauricio Gugelmin had failed to qualify.

The CG901 was the third Formula 1 car designed by Adrian Newey, the Briton who would go on to become *the* technical superstar of the modern age. He made his name at March Engineering, tinkering with and substantially lightening its GTP racer into a competitive prospect; that led to a deployment in the United States in 1983, where he redesigned March's Indy car into an altogether quicker device and also served as race engineer for Bobby Rahal. F1 beckoned, and in 1986 Newey left March to join the ailing FORCE team.

When FORCE shut down at the end of 1986, March immediately rehired Newey to work on its own F1 project. Newey's first design was the 881 of 1988, an aerodynamically innovative car that bore many of his hallmarks: a no-compromise approach to packaging, even if it made the drivers uncomfortable.

Its nose was so narrow in comparison to its rivals that to access the cockpit a driver had to align one leg on top of the other so that they could both pass through the structural hoop. Newey's reasoning was that with a modest, normally aspirated Judd V-8 supplying the power, the car had to be as slippery as possible.

The 881 looked striking in the turquoise colors of principal sponsor Leyton House, a Japanese real estate company. The car was a revelation in a season of McLaren dominance, becoming the only normally aspirated car to lead a race when Capelli briefly passed Ayrton Senna at Suzuka. But the team was a low-budget effort, and reliability was always a problem. At the end of 1988, March sold the team to its sponsor; under the flamboyant leadership of Akira Akagi, Leyton House had ridden the Japanese property boom and had ambitious plans to become an international luxury-goods empire.

But the 1989 car was unsuccessful, and at first the 1990 model wasn't much better. Once again, Newey had focused uncompromisingly on the wind-tunnel numbers, and his ideas were beyond the reach of the team's manufacturing capabilities. The CG901 was a pig to drive: It wasn't structurally rigid enough, and to make the aerodynamics work the suspension had to be set up so stiffly that even minor bumps threw the car off course. Its cockpit was like a second skin, and without power steering the drivers had little leverage on the tiny 25-centimeter wheel.

"Often, you couldn't change the steering angle once you were in a corner, especially the fast ones," said Capelli. "You just had to commit to the corner and hold the steering there, hoping you'd got the angle right and weren't just going to fly off the circuit."

For some time, all F1 cars had used a diffuser under the tail to channel air out from under the car, reducing drag and creating aerodynamic downforce that enabled them to corner quicker. But apart from that, they were flat-bottomed, all the way to the nose—and had been ever since the FIA mandated flat bottoms in the early 1980s. Newey had realized

that he could exploit the diffuser more effectively if he could improve the flow of air reaching it. So he raised the entire nose of the car and fitted a splitter plate under the driver's legs.

At first, the team couldn't understand why the CG901 wasn't working, a problem that was compounded when a power struggle erupted after team manager Ian Phillips contracted viral meningitis at the Brazilian GP. Various members of Akagi's entourage began to assert themselves, pointing the finger of blame at Newey.

But Newey had identified the principal failing: His numbers were wrong. The fiberglass working area of the team's rented wind tunnel was flexing, skewing the results. The CG901's diffuser was too aggressive—it would suck the rear of the car almost to the ground, stall, and immediately suck the car down again when the suspension had sprung back up.

A diffuser is a structural part of an F1 car's floor; it is not something one can simply bolt on. Newey designed a complete "B" spec of the CG901, including a new floor and diffuser and revised sidepods, but by the time the new car was ready for action—at the French GP—he had decided to move on; he negotiated a payoff and left, reappearing at Williams some weeks later.

Paul Ricard was a flat, fast circuit with a bump-free but abrasive surface that was hard on tires. Almost immediately, Capelli and his race engineer, Gustav Brunner, realized they had a chance of winning. Without any bumps to disrupt it, the CG901's new aero package was working perfectly.

The key to a quick lap at Paul Ricard was to be fast down the long main straight and then hold that speed through the two tightening corners that followed, Signes and Beausset. Capelli could take Signes flat out, but he and Brunner altered the setup of the car so that theoretically, if he lifted off a little before Signes, he would still be fast but gentle enough on the tires to last the race without a pit stop.

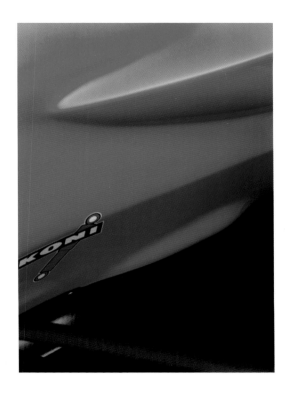

So close. . .yet: The CG901 nearly achieved the unthinkable at the 1990 French Grand Prix: Capelli, both mirrors still intact, holds off Prost in the waning laps. "I was thinking in the last five laps that winning was possible," Capelli later reflected. LAT Photographic

After a conservative start from seventh on the grid, Capelli stroked his CG901 around Ricard for the first half of the race, gaining a position each time someone ahead of him pitted. At half distance, he was leading, with teammate Gugelmin in second place. Gradually, Prost and Senna began to catch them. And then, disaster for Gugelmin: His car ground to a halt amid a haze of oil smoke.

Sensing victory, Prost was on Capelli's tail within a handful of laps. But he could not pass. Capelli had lost one of his mirrors, so when he reached the circuit's prime overtaking spot, he simply stamped on the brakes and turned in, not knowing whether Prost was there or not. Perhaps intimidated a little by this aggression, Prost held back.

Alas, the fairytale ending was not to be. Three laps from the end, Capelli's oil pump sheared off and, for just a few heart-rending minutes, he feared he wouldn't even finish. But he did—ahead of Senna. Two weeks after failing to qualify for one GP, he was standing on the podium of another.

Although Newey had outlined a 1991 car with active suspension and a sequential gearbox, his replacement elected to start from a clean sheet. Thus, the innovations Newey had pioneered at Leyton House transferred to Williams, which went on to win the drivers' title four times with Newey-designed cars. Soon, every team copied the raised-nose arrangement and every car had a cockpit like a second skin.

Leyton House quickly faded from the scene. Akagi's empire imploded in the Japanese economic crash, and the team closed in 1993.

What might have been: Prost celebrates while the expression on Capelli's face says it all. "Initially, I was so happy because I managed to finish. Then, one meter after the finish line, I realized I had lost a race I should have won. That's not a good feeling." LAT Photographic

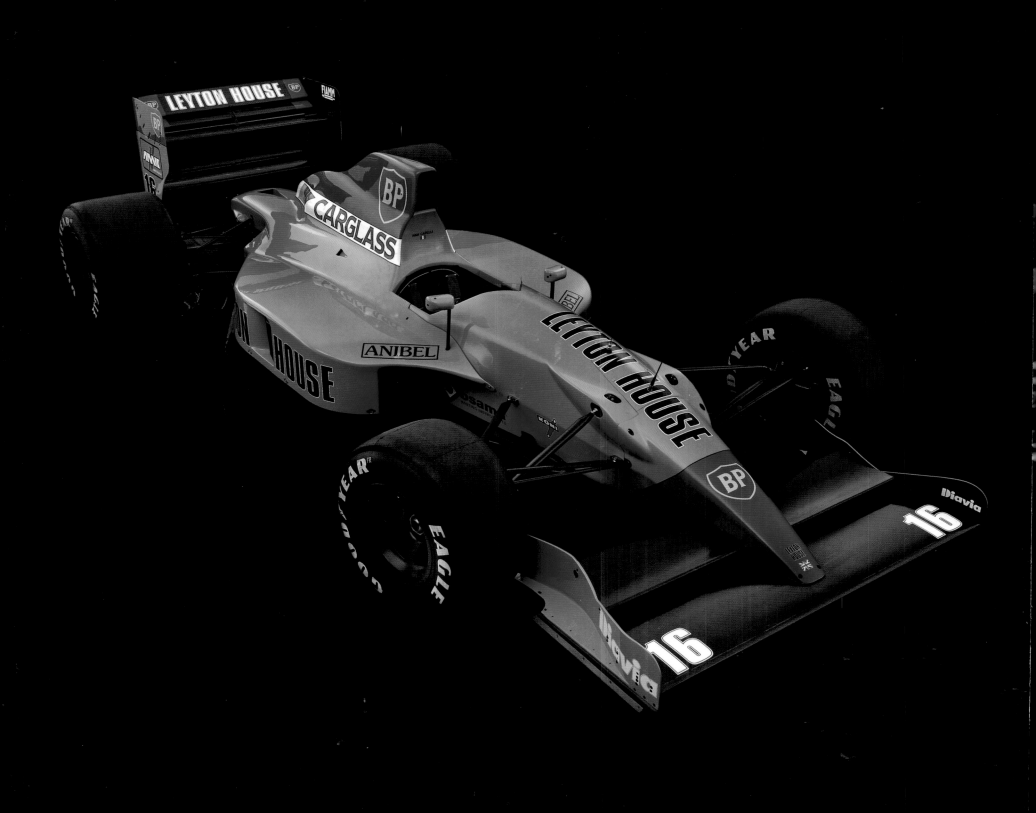

Leyton House CG901

First championship GP
U.S. (Phoenix), 1990

Last championship GP
Australia (Adelaide), 1990

Wins/championship races entered
0/16

Wins
None

Engine
3,496-cc Judd V-8, 640 horsepower (est.)

This is the turning point in Formula 1, where aerodynamics became so much more important than anything else—particularly now when there are large-scale wind tunnels that permit detailed work. From this era onward, aerodynamics took over.

Adrian Newey is an aerodynamicist. When I was designing F1 cars, I'd say, 'Okay, what's the fundamental holistic thing I'm trying to achieve? What am I looking for an improvement in?' And with Adrian, it's aerodynamic purity.

Gordon Murray

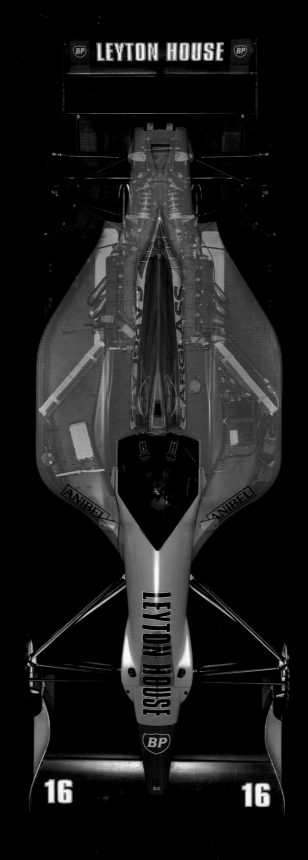

15

Jordan 191

EDDIE JORDAN ONCE WORKED IN A BANK. He was an entrepreneur—a wheeler-dealer, a chancer with the Irishman's gift of the gab. And he loved motor racing, graduating from being a moderately successful single-seater racer in the late 1970s to winning championships in the lower formulae as a team owner in the 1980s. But that wasn't enough. He wanted to be in Formula 1.

Gary Anderson was a phenomenally intuitive engineer and a big bear of a man who reputedly could heft a Cosworth DFV block by himself. After leaving the Brabham F1 team, he designed a series of successful Formula 3 cars in the 1980s, spent a few years in Indy cars, then returned to the U.K. as Reynard's chief designer on its Formula 3000 project. At the end of 1989, he fielded a phone call from Jordan, his old F3 sparring partner:

"I think I've got enough money to build an F1 car. Do you want to come and join me?"

Jordan hounded the initially skeptical Anderson into submission with a blizzard of phone calls, and on a typically bleak Silverstone day in February 1990, Anderson reported for duty at Jordan's industrial unit overlooking the circuit. His first job was to go out and buy some drawing boards, paper, French curves, rulers, and pencils.

As a new team, Jordan would have to pre-qualify—an ignominious and hurried procedure held on the Friday morning of the GP weekend whereby the slowest cars were ejected. Only the fastest four

Simple, elegant, quick: The Jordan 191 proved quick enough in the hands of Bertrand Gachot (pictured) and Andrea de Cesaris for the new team firstly to escape pre-qualifying, and then to irritate the "works" Ford team, Benetton. LAT Photographic

cars from the worst-performing teams on the grid made it through. It was necessary, given that there were often up to 40 entries and only 26 places on the grid, but it was also nasty. Drivers would often deliberately dawdle on the racing line after setting a hot lap to spoil things for their rivals.

Working with a staff of two other designers, Anderson outlined the 191 with minimal time in the wind tunnel (Jordan couldn't afford more), following the principle of simplicity. The team would not have the time in pre-qualifying to analyze the car's behavior in detail; it had to be quick out of the box, vice-free, and easy to set up.

Luck—both good and bad—would play an important role in the final phase of the 191's development. Having envisioned that the car would use the new Judd V-10 produced by Engine Developments, Anderson found himself lunching in a pub at the same time as Cosworth's Bernard Ferguson. From this encounter came an opportunity to use Ford's HB V-8 engine, albeit a unit some development steps behind the engine used by Benetton.

But Ford also persuaded Jordan's sponsor, Camel, to move to Benetton, since the works team appeared a better prospect. All of a sudden Jordan had a car—albeit one with a new bulge on the engine cover to accommodate Ford's taller V-8—but no sponsor. When Eddie Jordan showed the 191 to the world's press, it was still in black carbon fiber. Predictably, the reaction was negative.

"Why do they bother?" wrote journalist Jabby Crombac. "They can't even afford to paint the car."

But Eddie Jordan, the master wheeler-dealer, was always at his best when his back was against the wall. He signed a deal with the 7-Up beverage company that would enable him to paint the 191 in an appropriately Irish shade of green. And when this alienated another potential sponsor, Kodak, on the grounds that green was the

corporate color of arch-rival Fuji, Jordan got on a plane to Japan and talked Fuji into a deal. He was on a roll.

Jordan's drivers didn't inspire a great deal of confidence, but they did bring much-needed money. Andrea de Cesaris was no longer the crash-prone wild man he was in the early 1980s, but after a decade in F1 he had won nothing except a reputation for being obstreperous when lapped. Still, his family connections enabled him to tap the Marlboro purse. Bertrand Gachot had been runner-up in the British F3 championship in 1987 but had been too determined to race in F1 to be choosy about who he drove for; after two seasons of scratching about in cars barely good enough to pre-qualify, his profile was on the wane.

In fact, Gachot had already torpedoed his F1 career before the start of the 1991 season, although neither he nor anyone else realized it at the time. Eric Court is not a name that would otherwise figure in the annals of F1 history, except that in December 1990 his taxi and Gachot's Alfa Romeo were involved in a contretemps on London's Hyde Park Corner. Gachot had a CS gas canister in his car—for his girlfriend's protection, he claimed later—and in his fury, he discharged it in Court's face. Gachot's act was to have a profound effect both on his own career and the future of F1.

Although de Cesaris failed to pre-qualify for the first race of the 1991 season, Gachot ran competitively until his engine failed in the closing laps. Soon, the other teams realized that a threat was in their midst: De Cesaris and Gachot were running fourth and fifth in Mexico until Gachot spun off. Although reliability continued to be a problem (de Cesaris had to push his car over the line in Mexico), Jordan regularly finished in the top 10 and accrued enough points to escape pre-qualifying in the second half of the season.

Gachot and de Cesaris also pushed the Benetton pairing of Nelson Piquet (a three-time world champion, but now well into cruise-and-collect mode) and Roberto

Moreno hard enough for Jordan to put pressure on Ford for better engines. Flavio Briatore, the Benetton team principal, became increasingly disgruntled at the prospect of having his engine deal blarneyed out from under him.

Gachot set fastest lap at the Hungarian GP, albeit after a late change for new tires, but it was to be his last race for Jordan. When his road-rage case came to trial, he was jailed for 18 months. Eddie, in desperate need of someone to drive his car at the next race, the Belgian GP at Spa-Francorchamps, began casting around for a replacement driver—preferably a cheap one. He was approached by Mercedes, who wanted to give a young German sports car driver named Michael Schumacher some F1 experience.

Jordan was assured that Schumacher had raced at Spa before. He hadn't; he essayed his first lap of the legendary track on a bicycle the Thursday before the Grand Prix. Not that it mattered—Schumacher finished the first session eighth fastest and qualified seventh. He burned out his clutch at the start of the race but had done enough to demonstrate that he was a phenomenal talent. This race was arguably the 191's finest hour: Spurred on by Schumacher's turn of speed, de Cesaris found the pace to challenge Ayrton Senna for the lead until his engine blew.

But Schumacher would never sit in the 191's cockpit again. F1 politics is a nightmare territory of wheels within wheels; behind the scenes, between the Belgian and Italian GPs, deals were being done. Jordan believed he had a binding contract, or at least a letter of intent, for Schumacher to stay with his team. Instead, Eddie could only rail against the injustice of it all as Schumacher strode down the Monza paddock wearing Benetton overalls. He would win two world championships for that team and five more for Ferrari, dominating F1 for more than a decade.

McLaren boss Ron Dennis took Eddie aside. "Welcome to the Piranha Club," he said, sympathetically.

Yes, Eddie Jordan had arrived in Formula 1.

At first, Eddie Jordan was more interested in the wad of Mercedes cash that accompanied Michael Schumacher (pictured) than the young German's driving abilities. And then Schumacher qualified seventh in his first Grand Prix. . . . *LAT Photographic*

Jordan 191

First championship GP
U.S. (Phoenix), 1971

Last championship GP
Australia (Adelaide), 1991

Wins/championship races entered
0/16

Wins
None

Engine
3,493-cc Ford V-8, 640 horsepower (est.)

" *Gary Anderson was my chief mechanic for years and years. It's no wonder this is such an intuitive piece of design. Our early Brabhams didn't go near a wind tunnel; everything was done with wool tufts stuck on the cars at tests. Gary would have been comfortable designing it by eye with limited tunnel time. It's very balanced and elegant— and beautifully simple.* "

Gordon Murray

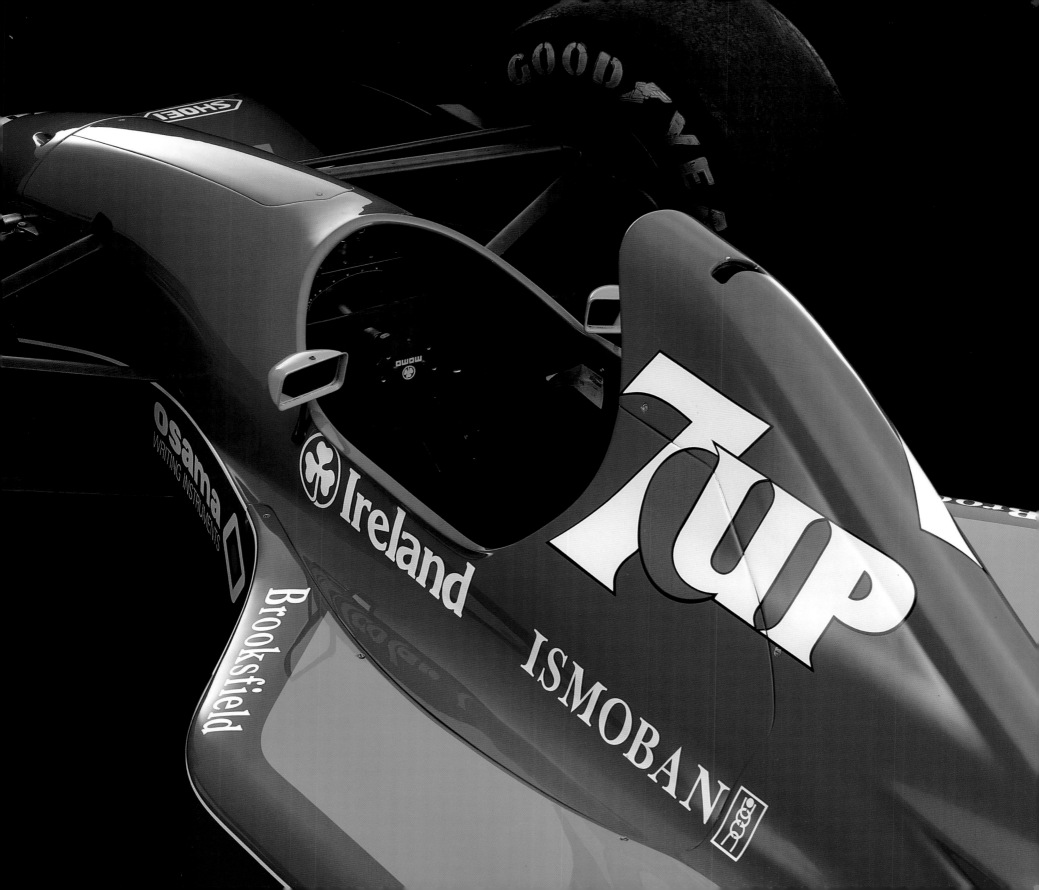

16
Williams FW14

FEW FORMULA 1 TEAM OWNERS ARE
as intimately acquainted as Frank Williams with
the abrupt swings in competitiveness the sport can
bring. From a position of outright dominance in the
mid-1980s, his team plunged to the back of the grid
when Honda decided to transfer its V-6 turbo engines
to McLaren in 1988—and all because Williams
had refused to replace Nigel Mansell with Satoru
Nakajima, a middling Japanese driver who enjoyed
Honda patronage.

Mansell, a combative and often difficult person
both inside the cockpit and out, was a remarkable
driver. Drama attended his career like a Greek chorus.
His path to F1 had been difficult: He'd broken his
neck in a Formula Ford accident, quit a full-time
job and sold most of his worldly goods to finance
his racing career, but still had been given the cold
shoulder by the F1 industry until Peter Windsor
brought him to Colin Chapman's attention. Mansell
proved his speed and grittiness at Lotus before moving
on to Williams, where he almost but not quite won
the drivers' championship—twice. And then, after
that miserable 1988 season with stopgap Judd V-8
engines, he departed for Ferrari.

Frank swiftly rebuilt, acquiring an exclusive
supply of Renault V-10 engines for 1989. Bolted
into an evolution of the 1988 FW12 chassis, the new
engine delivered an instant uplift in competitiveness,
including a one-two finish at the Canadian GP; but
still, some vital spark seemed to be missing.

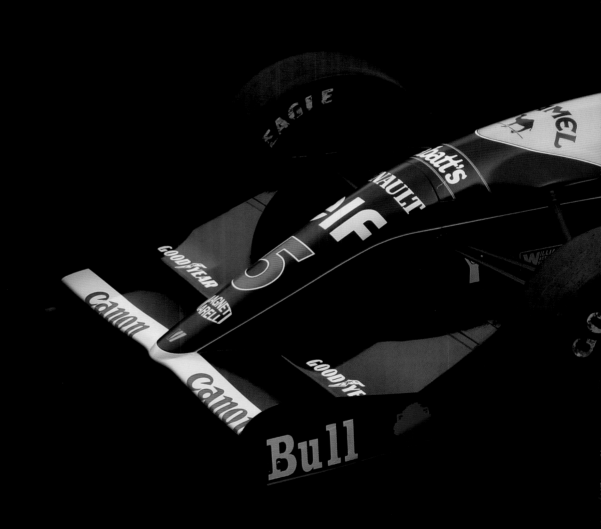

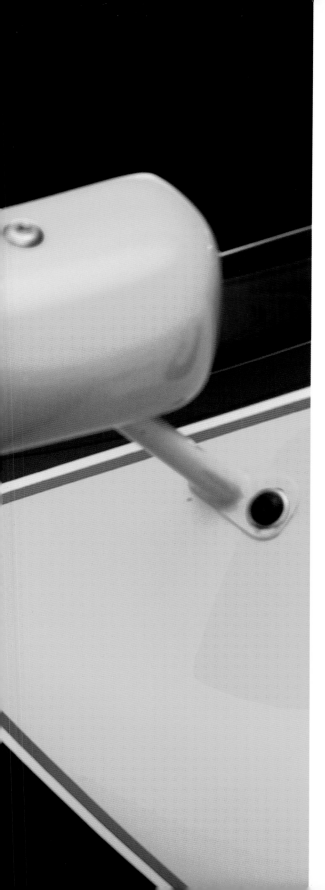

Mansell testing the FW14 in February 1991. The new car was finished late, and only hit the track for the first time a month before the start of the season. Glitches with its semi-automatic gearbox would cost Nigel Mansell a shot at the 1991 title. Williams F1 Team

Meanwhile, Mansell had been driven to despair at Ferrari by the unreliability of his car and the politicking of his teammate, the 1989 world champion Alain Prost. After retiring from the British GP in 1990, Mansell stormed back to the paddock and announced his permanent retirement from motor racing to the world's press.

"I can't say much," he growled, "but what I will say is. . . ." Journalists had long since learned that when Mansell uttered these words it was their cue to activate their tape recorders.

Mansell's retirement was one of the shortest phases of his career. A little over seven months later, in late February 1991, he was shaking down the Williams FW14 at Silverstone. Despite slithering off the wet track and ending up axle-deep in mud, he was enthusiastic: "I'm putting everything into 1991," he said. "And I'm even talking 1992." He was 37 years old; clearly, the new Williams car, though very late (the shakedown took place just over two weeks before the start of the season), had massive potential.

Mechanically and aerodynamically, the FW14 shared very little with its predecessors. It enjoyed considerable input from the team's new chief designer, Adrian Newey, and in the profile of its tapered, low-slung sidepods, raised nose, V-shaped cockpit aperture, and tightly packaged rear, it bore a family resemblance to the Leyton House CG901. The front wing was slightly raised in the middle, and the endplates extended back around the front wheels. The shock absorbers were mounted horizontally rather than vertically.

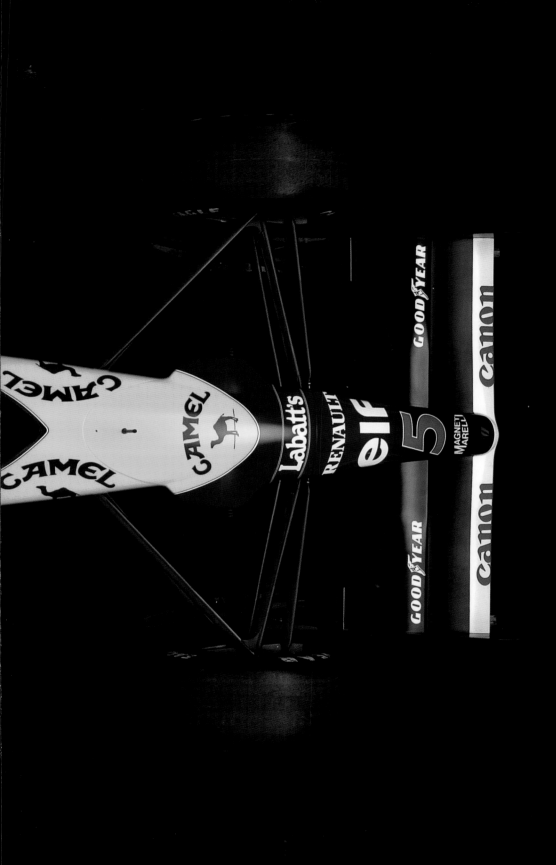

The alliance of Newey's creativity and technical director Patrick Head's experience produced a sweet-handling and aero-efficient racing car; and in Renault's V-10, it had one of the most powerful engines on the grid. A better-packaged one, too: The RS3 V-10 was 17 millimeters lower than the RS2. The FW14's only potential weak spot was its new semi-automatic gearbox.

The chief opposition in 1991 would not be Ferrari, which had flattered to deceive by setting quick times in winter testing, but McLaren-Honda. Over the winter, Ayrton Senna had made public his misgivings about the competitiveness of Honda's new V-12, which he said wasn't any more powerful than the V-10. One would never describe McLaren as complacent, but the team had enjoyed a power advantage for so long that its cars had perhaps become less aerodynamically efficient; certainly the MP4/6, with its big front and rear wings, did little to dispel this notion.

The season unfolded in a dramatic and often peculiar fashion. Senna won the first four races, building a safe cushion of championship points. The FW14 had race-winning pace, but Williams struggled to overcome glitches with the semi-automatic gearbox; Riccardo Patrese, in the twilight of his career, found a second wind and was often as quick as (or quicker than) Mansell, taking three consecutive pole positions.

Soon, though, Mansell began to assert himself—as did his demons. Drama was never far away: Having built an unassailable lead in the Canadian GP, Mansell began waving to the crowd on the last lap and missed a downshift; his engine shut down, and he ground to a halt almost within sight of the finishing line. During the Portuguese GP, his pit crew failed to attach one of his rear wheels properly, and as he drove off it departed on a different trajectory. And finally, having hauled himself back into championship contention, he speared off the track and into the gravel at Suzuka while chasing Senna.

An exhausted Mansell takes a breather after a typically tigerish display in Monaco, 1992. A puncture cost him the lead but he harried eventual winner Ayrton Senna over the closing laps. Williams F1 Team

The FW14B's active suspension robbed the driver of feel, but Mansell's dogged bravura enabled him to tame the car, whatever the conditions. Here, in the wet at Barcelona in 1992, he won by a margin of 27 seconds. Williams F1 Team

Over the winter, Newey refined the FW14's aerodynamics, and Renault arrived at a still more powerful evolution of the V-10. For 1992, the "B" spec of the FW14 would also feature a technology Williams had tried—and discarded on reliability grounds—in 1988: active suspension. The system involved some extra bulk (on the FW14B pictured here, you can see the bulges on each side where the pushrods enter the nose) but enabled the aerodynamics to work at maximum efficiency by keeping the car flat, relative to the road, eliminating the variations of pitch and roll.

"We like our technology at Williams," Head told the press in January, "but we don't go racing with these gizmos for the sake of it. I've never believed we could beat McLaren by running a more reliable car, by operating it better—no, the only way to beat them is by building a car that's plain *faster*. And all this trick stuff—active ride, semi-automatic gearbox, and so on—should make things easier and less tiring for the drivers, as well as making the car quicker."

Mansell won the first five Grands Prix of 1992. He could have won all of them; Patrese couldn't keep up. More often than not, the FW14Bs would finish one-two, at least a lap ahead of anyone else. Only the intervention of fate—in the form of bad luck and mechanical unreliability—prevented Mansell from winning more. He had the championship sewn up by the Hungarian GP, race 11 of 16.

And yet even in Mansell's hour of triumph, the soap opera wasn't far away. A veritable conga line of talented drivers was forming outside Williams HQ, with Alain Prost at its head. Mansell couldn't countenance being Prost's teammate again—he quit Formula 1 for Indy car racing.

Predictably, active suspension became a must-have, along with traction control and many other electronic aids that many fans felt detracted from the spectacle of Formula 1. The FIA stepped in to ban them, and F1 will never see the likes of the FW14 again.

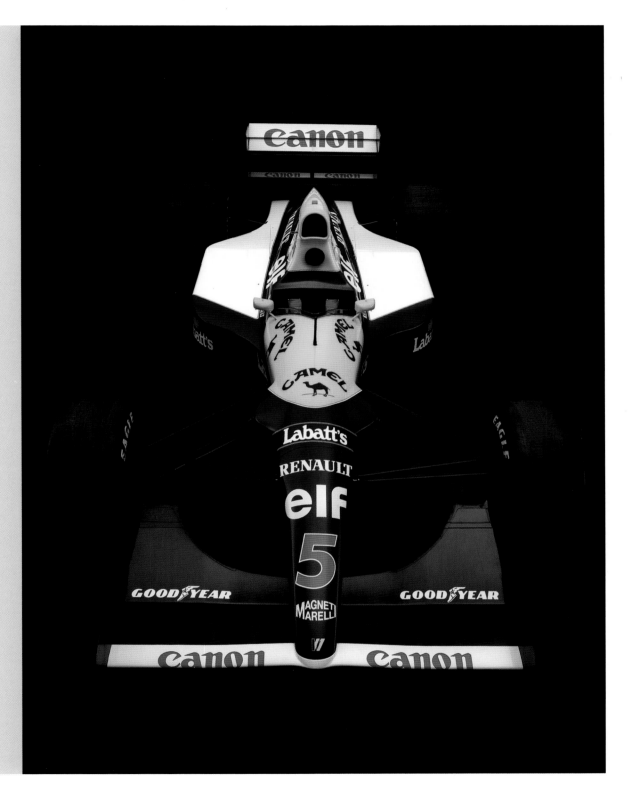

*" You can see the family resemblance to the
Leyton House, the clean aero. With that, and
all that power and all the electronics, it's no
wonder it was pretty much untouchable. "*

Gordon Murray

I was out of Formula 1 by the time this car raced. And thank God I was; that time was just such a dead end for F1. That direction—active suspension, traction control, and so on—it was totally the wrong thing to do. It was never going to lead anywhere, except to pain and tears and complication, and too many failures in the races for spectators. It took too much away from the spectacle.

Gordon Murray

Williams FW14

First championship GP
U.S. (Phoenix), 1991

Last championship GP
Australia (Adelaide), 1992

Wins/championship races entered
17/32

Wins

Mexico (Mexico City)	1991	Patrese
France (Magny-Cours)	1991	Mansell
Great Britain (Silverstone)	1991	Mansell
Germany (Hockenheim)	1991	Mansell
Italy (Monza)	1991	Mansell
Portugal (Estoril)	1991	Patrese
Spain (Barcelona)	1991	Mansell
South Africa (Kyalami)	1992	Mansell
Mexico (Mexico City),	1992	Mansell
Brazil (Interlagos)	1992	Mansell
Spain (Barcelona)	1992	Mansell
San Marino (Imola),	1992	Mansell
France (Magny-Cours)	1992	Mansell
Great Britain (Silverstone)	1992	Mansell
Germany (Hockenheim)	1992	Mansell
Portugal (Estoril)	1992	Mansell
Japan (Suzuka)	1992	Patrese

Engine
3,493-cc Renault V-10, 740 horsepower (est.)

Ferrari
F1-2000

WHEN JODY SCHECKTER CLINCHED THE
1979 drivers' title for Ferrari, narrowly beating
teammate Gilles Villeneuve, even a hardened
pessimist would not have predicted that another 21
years and over 340 races would pass before a Ferrari
driver hoisted the championship trophy again. The
interregnum is a sorry tale of petty politics, squan-
dered promise, and a revolving-door management
structure, finally resolved by the arrival of some of
the finest racing brains of the modern era.

Alain Prost came close to glory in 1990 with
the V-12-engined 641 designed by John Barnard; but
Barnard left to join Benetton, and his successors failed
to evolve the 641 competitively. Prost then fell out
with management to the extent that he was sacked
(after saying the 643 drove like a truck), and the team
plunged into the doldrums again, cranking through
designers and management at a pace as successive cars
failed to deliver the goods.

FIAT, Ferrari's owner, brought Luca
Montezemolo back in 1991, and in 1993 he poached
Jean Todt from Peugeot to run the team and tempted
Barnard back to design the car. Barnard, a known
quantity, was able to name his terms, which included
being allowed to operate from an office near Guildford
in the U.K. Todt, who had moved to Maranello after
masterminding Peugeot's success in rallying and
sports cars, rapidly wondered why he'd bothered.

"As soon as I walked into the Ferrari building,"
he recalled, "I saw that everything had been *damaged*."

The unremitting hostility might have broken a lesser man. His house was burglarized, and he was subjected to torrents of abuse in the Italian media. One day, he came home to find a broken pair of scissors on his pillow. But Todt was made of sterner stuff than his predecessors. He set about revolutionizing Ferrari from the inside, weathering the criticism when results weren't instantly forthcoming, and for the 1996 season he staged a remarkable coup: signing world champion Michael Schumacher away from Benetton, followed within the year by Benetton's technical director and chief designer, Ross Brawn and Rory Byrne. Barnard decided to quit rather than relocate to Italy.

Brawn arrived to find a dispersed design office; for years, Barnard had filed his designs by fax, one sheet of paper at a time, which had then to be assembled with tape into a complicated patchwork blueprint. In contrast, Paulo Martinelli's engine department was ticking over smoothly.

Still, rebuilding the team—recruiting new engineers and aerodynamicists, and putting new management structures in place—took time. Williams dominated the 1997 season, McLaren in 1998 and 1999; every time, Ferrari had a small but significant performance deficit that only Schumacher could regularly overcome.

The F1-2000 was a completely new car, designed around a new engine with a V-angle that had been opened out from 80 to 89 degrees, providing a lower center of gravity and enabling the aerodynamicists (working for the first time in Ferrari's new wind tunnel) to package the rear more tightly. Schumacher won the first three races of the 2000 season, demonstrating that the F1-2000 could match McLaren's MP4/15 on pace while beating it for reliability.

And when the McLarens did run reliably, Brawn and Schumacher outmaneuvered them on guile alone. At the San Marino GP, Mika Hakkinen had a three-second lead over Schumacher when he pitted for fuel; Brawn opted to put extra fuel in at

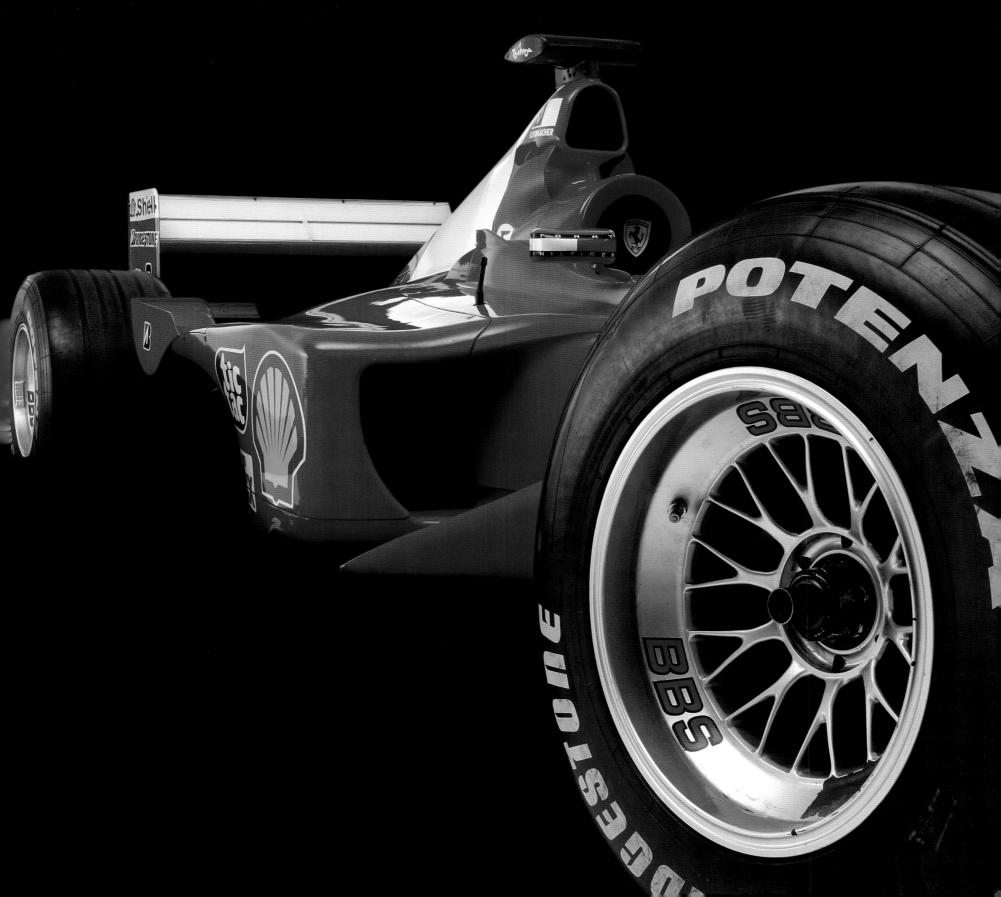

Schumacher's stop, enabling him to run a longer middle stint. Schumacher paced himself exquisitely, sitting a couple of seconds behind Hakkinen until the second and final round of pit stops. When Hakkinen peeled in, Schumacher erupted forward, reeling off a sequence of laps so quick that he emerged from his own pit stop still in the lead.

The F1-2000 wasn't quite perfect; winter testing had lulled the designers into expecting the tires to be harder, so the rear suspension was rather too flexible and prone to hurting its Bridgestones. And its engine was running so lean—for fuel economy purposes—that it was operating at the limits of its duty cycle. At Monaco, Schumacher lost the win when his left exhaust failed and the subsequent flame-outs destroyed an upper wishbone. During the mid-season, his championship lead over McLaren's David Coulthard evaporated after he failed to finish in France, Austria, and Germany.

Michael finally sealed the drivers' title at the penultimate race of the season, on that quintessential drivers' circuit: Suzuka. It was another masterly tactical display by Brawn and Schumacher, wrongfooting the McLarens just as they had done at Imola.

Ferrari was at last a devastatingly effective fighting unit: a team united under the leadership of Todt and Schumacher, who seemed as close as father and son. Together with Brawn and Byrne, they would dominate the first decade of the new millennium, winning every drivers' championship through 2004. Schumacher inspired the utter devotion of the Ferrari crew and even won over the Italian public.

And when the partnership broke up in 2006—Todt to a senior position within the wider Ferrari empire, Byrne and Schumacher to semi-retirement, and Brawn to a sabbatical—the lieutenants they had groomed for so long simply stepped forward and continued the tradition of success, utterly seamlessly—something that would have been unthinkable 20, or even 10, years earlier.

Schumacher and the F1-2000 on song in the wet at the 2000 European Grand Prix at the Nürburgring, where the German would score the fourth of nine victories that season. *LAT Photographic*

Team manager Jean Todt led Ferrari out of the doldrums and formed a championship-winning partnership with Michael Schumacher. *LAT Photographic*

> *It was after this car that, for me, F1 cars started getting ugly. Even the bargeboards on this are relatively pretty. Relatively—I don't like bargeboards, although I can see why they're absolutely necessary.*
>
> *Gordon Murray*

Ferrari F1-2000

First championship GP
Australia (Albert Park), 2000

Last championship GP
Malaysia (Sepang), 2000

Wins/championship races entered
10/17

Wins

Australia (Albert Park)	2000	Schumacher
Brazil (Interlagos)	2000	Schumacher
San Marino (Imola)	2000	Schumacher
Europe (Nürburgring)	2000	Schumacher
Canada (Montreal)	2000	Schumacher
Germany (Hockenheim)	2000	Rubens Barrichello
Italy (Monza)	2000	Schumacher
U.S. (Indianapolis)	2000	Schumacher
Japan (Suzuka)	2000	Schumacher
Malaysia (Sepang)	2000	Schumacher

Engine
2,996-cc Ferrari V-10, 780 horsepower (est.)

18
McLaren MP4-23

THAT FORMULA 1 IS A HUMAN DRAMA as well as a technical battle is demonstrated graphically by the story of the McLaren MP4-23. Rarely can a racing car have been designed in such a poisonous political climate of suspicion, antipathy, and rancor. Before the car had even turned a wheel on track, its lead driver and engineering director were cross-examined in court, and the team that built it was handed a staggering $100 million fine for its conduct in an espionage scandal that had shaken the sport.

Early in 2007, before the first MP4-23 models had seen the wind tunnel, ambition led McLaren's chief designer, Mike Coughlan, to a catastrophic error of judgment. He obtained technical secrets from Nigel Stepney, formerly Ferrari's race technical manager but lately transferred to a nebulous factory-bound role at Maranello. Why? Stepney, by all accounts, coveted the technical director position at Ferrari recently vacated by Ross Brawn; Coughlan, similarly, wanted more say in the technical direction at McLaren.

The world might never have known about this act of corporate espionage had Coughlan not made an arguably even more catastrophic error of judgment: He sent his wife to a local photocopying shop to have the documents duplicated. One of the shop's employees immediately recognized the Ferrari logo and tipped off Ferrari management. The surreal story went public, and the accusations began to fly.

At first, McLaren claimed that Coughlan had been working alone and that few other McLaren

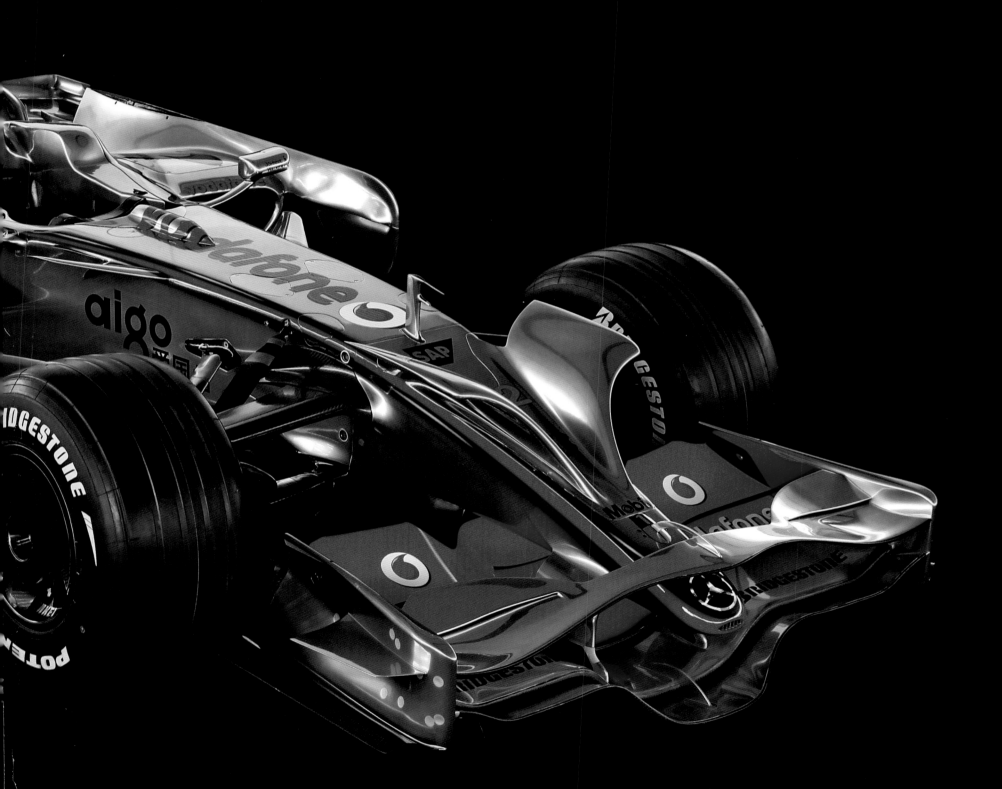

employees had seen the Ferrari documents. McLaren claimed that its design office's flat, matrix management structure had prevented the Ferrari information from spreading through the organization. But as the story developed from a trickle into a highly damaging torrent of revelations in the summer of 2007, it became clear that knowledge of Ferrari's secrets had percolated more deeply through the organization than McLaren had admitted at first, and for that it was punished to the tune of $100 million by the FIA's World Motor Sport Council (WMSC) on September 13, 2007.

Even that wasn't to be the end of the matter. The genesis of the MP4-23, McLaren's 2008 car, became the focus of scrutiny. FIA inspectors visited the McLaren Technology Centre to examine the designs for any element that could have been influenced by knowledge of Ferrari's systems. Finally—after a soul-baring public apology from McLaren—the FIA declared the matter closed in a statement issued on December 13, 2007, canceling a meeting of the WMSC planned for February 14, 2008, to discuss the MP4-23's legality.

The press, of course, continued to hound the team, and at the launch of the MP4-23 in January, the Italian media had clearly been briefed to ask about the car's wheelbase (longer than the MP4-22's). Only when the racing began in earnest did questions about the MP4-23's provenance begin to abate—and then only because Ferrari seemed to have the upper hand. Although Lewis Hamilton, McLaren's young superstar, won the opening Grand Prix, Ferrari's Kimi Räikkönen won the next race by some margin. Hamilton seemed rattled and continued to commit serious blunders: He botched the start in Bahrain and drove into the back of Räikkönen in the pit lane in Canada.

The 2008 season developed into a fascinating technical battle between McLaren and Ferrari, challenged occasionally by BMW and Renault. Like its Ferrari counterpart, the MP4-23 was a nuanced evolution of its predecessor. The longer wheelbase was intended to make it less aggressive on its tires

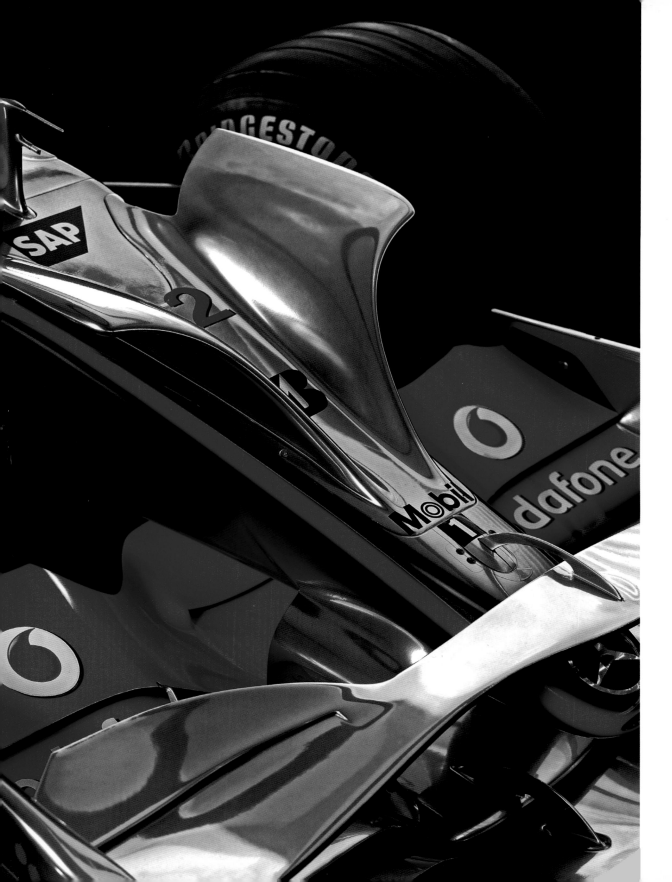

Technically and aerodynamically, this is unbelievably sophisticated. This car is a study in detailed aerodynamic design; it's not a holistic racing car. You could slice it up like a loaf of bread, and each part would have massive, focused, attention to detail—which then has to be integrated back into the total airflow. But even so, something like the wing endplate would have had one or two people working on it for a month.

Gordon Murray

197

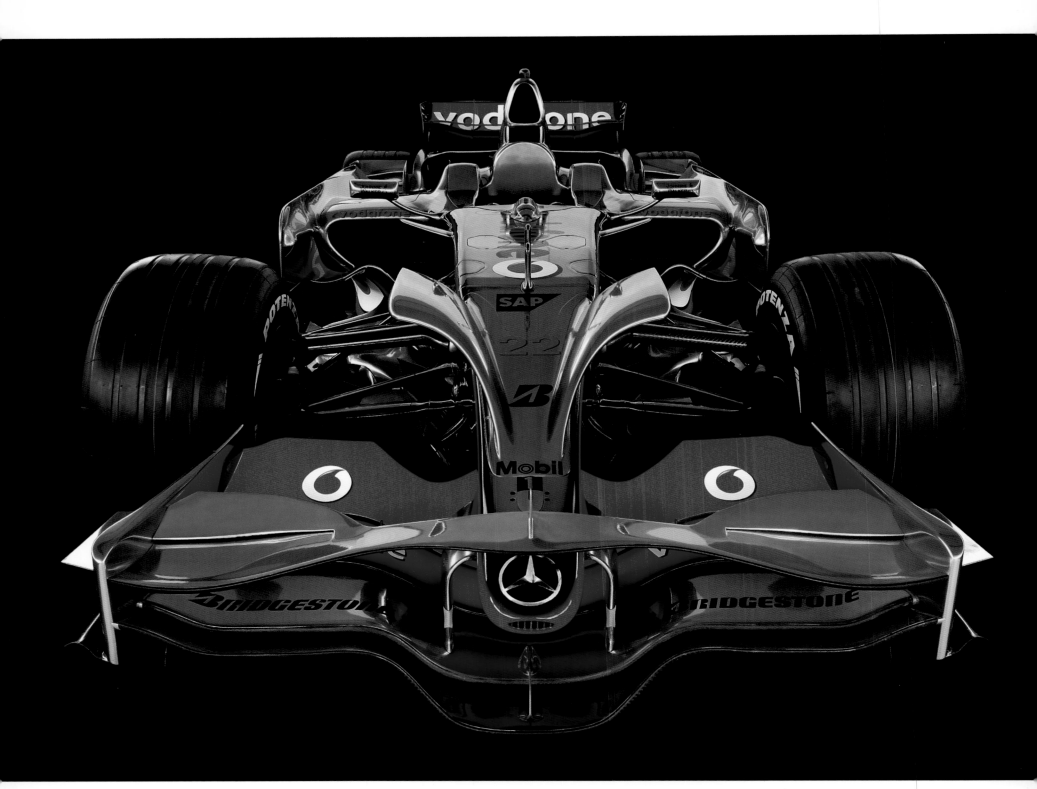

After almost a decade of domination by Michael Schumacher, interest in Formula 1 in the UK was waning until Lewis Hamilton arrived on the scene in 2007. *LAT Photographic*

In one of the defining races of his championship year, Hamilton utterly destroyed the opposition in the wet during his home Grand Prix at Silverstone. *Daimler*

than the MP4/22 (in combination with Hamilton's taste for an oversteering setup, this had made the rear tires marginal in 2007). Elsewhere, the emphasis was on easy tunability, for electronic driver aids such as traction control had been banned.

The MP4-23 was a masterpiece of aerodynamic detailing, possibly the finest of the aero-optimization era. (As of 2009, the rules were changed, outlawing many of the graceful flip-up wings and flow conditioners in the name of reduced costs and more overtaking.) The four-plane front wing seen at many races sacrificed some downforce-generating area but was less sensitive to changes in pitch; during the second half of the season, the team replaced the high-mounted bridge wing with an arcing pair of nose-mounted flow conditioners. These didn't contribute to overall downforce levels but assisted the airflow to the rear wing.

The dramatic and attritional season came down to the final race, the Brazilian GP at the Interlagos circuit in São Paolo, Brazil. The event provided a sensational denouement that redefined the cliché "nail-biting." The title race had come down to Hamilton versus Ferrari's Felipe Massa—a young Brazilian whom some had written off as a crash-prone nontalent earlier in his career. Coming into the race, Hamilton held a seven-point lead in the points table. To steal the championship, Massa would have to win the race and pray that Hamilton placed an unlikely sixth or lower. But what seemed like a foregone conclusion became more gripping as São Paulo–native Massa took pole position in front of his home crowd while Hamilton, encumbered by a more conservative fuel load, qualified fourth. A sharp downpour just before the start of the race raised the stakes further.

Massa duly shot off into an unassailable lead while a record-breaking global TV audience remained glued to Hamilton's progress. He slipped to seventh at the first round of pit stops, then recovered to fourth. As the laps ticked by, it looked like the young Briton had done just enough. But there was to be a succession of twists in the tale: Eight laps

Following the 2008 Brazilian Grand Prix, a euphoric Lewis Hamilton celebrates his world championship after the most tense and confusing climax to a race in F1 history. LAT Photographic

from the end, the rain came again. The leading runners pitted for intermediate wet-weather tires, but Toyota opted to roll the strategic dice and leave Jarno Trulli and Timo Glock out on dry-weather tires, a decision that allowed Glock to advance from seventh to fourth place.

Hamilton emerged from his pit stop in fifth place—still enough for the championship—but he scrabbled for grip and soon fell into the clutches of the Toro Rosso of Sebastian Vettel, who romped past Hamilton with three laps to go. The crowd, cheering on their home hero, roared approval from beneath their umbrellas.

Vettel left Hamilton sliding in his wake. The world over, trembling fingers grasped betting slips and prepared to tear them asunder. But this race wasn't over, and Glock proved to be the unlikely kingmaker: On the last lap, the rain intensified and all vestiges of grip disappeared. At the front of the field, Massa punched the air in triumph as he took the checkered flag; but 20 seconds down the road, the championship story was going into reverse once again. As Glock fought to keep his Toyota on the track around Juncao bend, almost within sight of the finish line, Vettel and Hamilton came slithering past him on the inside line, demoting him to sixth. And so Hamilton crossed the line in fifth place; for a moment, both he and his championship rival struggled to assimilate the radio messages their teams were sending them. Hamilton was champion. Massa's charge had cruelly fallen short by a single point.

Back in the pits, Massa unbelted himself, bowed to the crowd, and wearily climbed the stairs to the podium as TV cameramen and photographers sprinted down the pit lane in search of the fifth-placed man, now the youngest-ever Formula 1 world champion. For Massa, blinking back tears and heroically magnanimous in defeat, this was perhaps the defining step in his journey to manhood, to becoming a complete Grand Prix driver. For Lewis Hamilton, it was the consummation of over a decade's effort—and the beginning of the rest of his life.

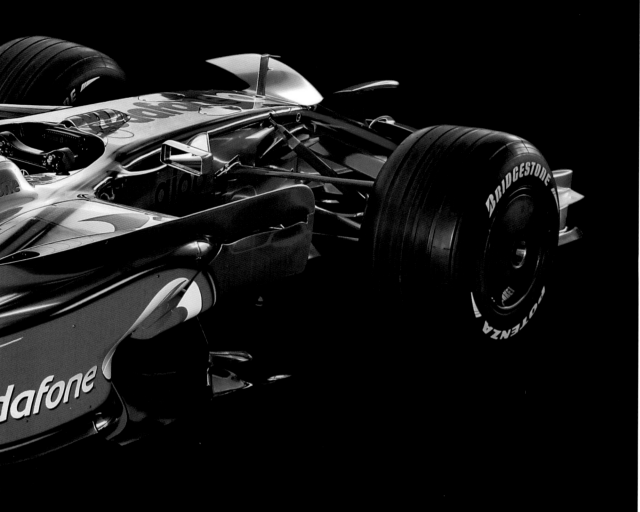

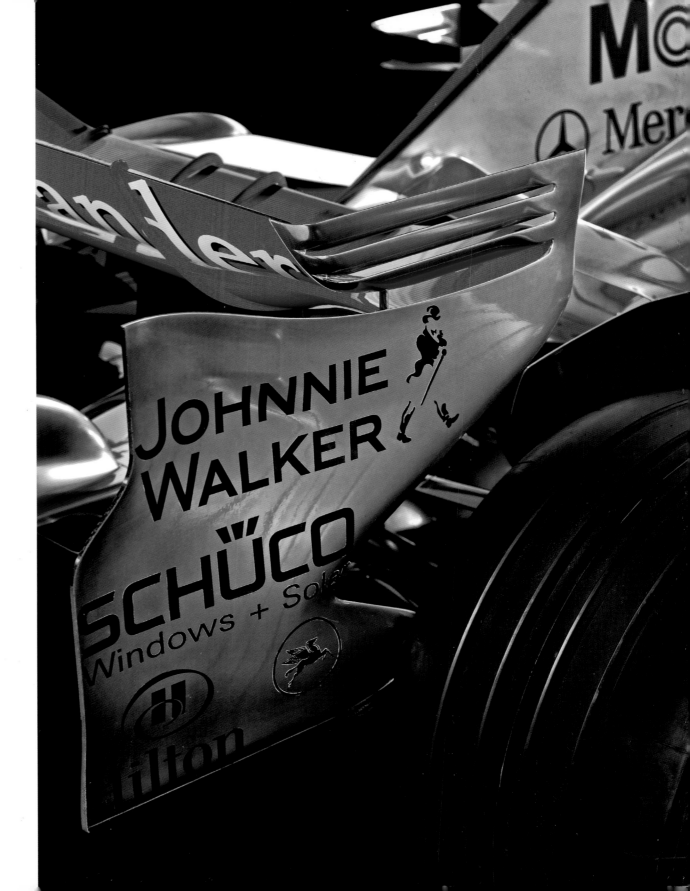

McLaren MP4-23

First championship GP
Australia (Melbourne), 2008

Last championship GP
Brazil (Interlagos), 2008

Wins/championship races entered
6/18

Wins

Brazil (Interlagos)	2008	Hamilton
Monaco (Monte Carlo)	2008	Hamilton
Britain (Silverstone)	2008	Hamilton
Germany (Hockenheim)	2008	Hamilton
Hungary (Hungaroring)	2008	Kovalainen
China (Shanghai)	2008	Hamilton

Engine
2,398cc Mercedes-Benz V-8, 780 horsepower (est.)

Photographer's Notes

BY JAMES MANN

TECHNOLOGY IS A WONDERFUL THING. I learned my trade in the days of film and Polaroid in the studio, using large-format 4x5-inch cameras; if you were lucky, you might manage five shots in a day. This book could not have happened had it not been for a new, affordable big-chip digital camera that appeared for the first time right at the start of this project.

Using the Canon 5DMkII with its 21 MP quality meant that we could shoot fantastic-quality images fast, sometimes fitting three full shoots into a day—a schedule that was necessary to match our budget constraints.

I decided early on to use a black background to allow the car to stand out and fulfill the "art" concept of the book. This was very important: Although many of these cars have been seen before, some even in the studio, none have been taken from an art perspective; we needed them to have a very different look. This was achieved by taking the cars away from their familiar environment at the track and placing them in the studio, allowing the reader to view them in a different light.

All the studios we used were white or gray infinity coves where the floor meets the walls and the walls meet the ceiling in a seamless curve. They are often used for advertising car shoots and pop videos, and when lit become ethereal spaces without horizons, a blank canvas on which to project an image and precisely control the subject.

I always use Arri tungsten movie lighting, as it offers the tremendous control in focusing needed for accurate attention to detail. This meant that exposures were long—typically 20 seconds—to achieve the depth of field required. A heavy studio stand was essential to lock off the camera.

A wall about one-meter high was built across the back of the studio, with lighting behind it and black cloth draped over it and around the car. Lighting was then directed from the camera with the assistant focusing, panning, and moving the lights to get the best effect.

Best results are usually achieved with the fewest number of lights, so we frequently went round before shooting, seeing which heads we could turn off so as to simplify the setup.

The overhead shots are always difficult. There must be enough height in the studio and preferably a camera mounting point above the cove. It is essential that the camera is exactly above the center of the car and everything is symmetrical. This is done by lowering a bob weight on a piece of string from the camera and positioning the car centrally below.

In studios where the ceiling was too low, we shot remotely with the camera fixed up on a lighting stand tethered to a laptop. Focusing, aperture, and shutter operation were all controlled from the computer with a live view through the lens.

Back in the office, we processed the digital images using Adobe Photoshop; we retouched the black to even out the color and smooth out the creases. We were mindful not to cut them out and place the cars on a created background, as this often looks clunky, but to use the existing black, which appears more sympathetic.

Camera and lenses:
Canon EOS 5DMkII, 20-35mm Canon F2.8, 50mm Canon F2.8, 70-200mm Canon F2.8

Acknowledgments

WHEN THE IDEA OF THIS BOOK came up, we knew it wouldn't be easy to do. Once we had convinced owners of the need to shoot in the studio, we then had to work out the logistics of how to get the cars to the three studio locations scattered around the UK.

We might have stalled had it not been for the generosity of James Hanson at Speedmaster cars in Bradford, who not only lent us his transporter, but also his driver, Andrew Thompson. James' good relationship with the Donington Grand Prix Exhibition was also essential to the project; we benefitted enormously from their mutual trust. Which leads on to Donington: our thanks to Kevin Wheatcroft and Neil Leavesley, both of whom took an active interest in the book from the start. We cemented the deal during a quick tour around the collection: When Stuart started recounting stories, facts, and figures about nearly every car in the displays, they could see we were serious.

A great friend and mentor over the years, John Colley, let us use his studio in Derby, which was close enough to Donington to allow us to shoot two cars in a day. John even came in one evening to test out the overhead rig with his own car to make sure it would work. For all his encouragement and support, we cannot thank him enough.

I must also thank my good buddy and ace studio assistant Jonathan Topps for his patience with me and optimism when it seemed as if we were up against it.

First to step up to the plate with the offer of a car was Mercedes with the W196 Streamliner; the pure fact that we shot this car first bolstered other owners to get involved with the book.

Last, but no means least, thanks go to Stuart Codling, as well as the publishers at Motorbooks, with whom I have photographed many books before but never with such enthusiastic and positive encouragement and support. Thanks especially to Motorbooks editor Jeff Zuehlke, whose spark got the ball rolling, and Motorbooks publisher Zack Miller, who picked it up and ran with it.

The Studios:

Plough Studios
Junction Eleven
John Colley Studios
Phoenix Green Studios

Thanks to:

Steve Cooper, Matt Bishop, and Ian Gosling at McLaren International. Natasha Barot, assistant for the London shoots. Liaz Jakhara at Zul racing who shifted the 7-foot 2-inch wide Jordan when no one else could. And the many others, too numerous to mention, who helped to transport the cars and put the book together. Finally, to my ever-patient family, Sarah, Rebecca, and Alex, who put up with my ups and downs. Thank you, all.

—James Mann, 2009

Thanks to:

James Mann, for his contagious enthusiasm throughout the project; Matt Bishop, for helping me into Formula 1 all those years ago; Peter Windsor, for his support and inspiration; Liam Clogger, Steve Cooper, Kevin Wheatcroft, and Jonathan Williams for taking such good care of these marvelous machines and furnishing us with access to them; Tiffany Hutt, for fitting us in at such a busy time; Kevin Wood, for arranging access to the LAT Archive and reserving the Jim Clark mug; and, finally, to the long-suffering Julie.

—Stuart Codling, 2009

The Cars:

Alfa Romeo 158/159	*Jim Stokes Workshops*
Maserati 250F	*Coys of Kensington/Chris Routledge*
Mercedes-Benz W196	*Florijan Hadjic and Daimler*
Lancia D50	*Tom Wheatcroft's Donington Grand Prix Collection*
BRM P57	*David Clark*
Brabham BT20	*Autofocusimages*
Lotus 49B	*Tom Wheatcroft's Donington Grand Prix Collection*
Lotus 72	*Clive Chapman at Classic Team Lotus*
Tyrrell 003	*Tom Wheatcroft's Donington Grand Prix Collection*
Tyrrell P34	*Simon Bull and Martin Stretton at historicracing.com*
Ferrari 312T3	*Mike Hallowes and Ten Tenths*
Williams FW07	*Jonathan Williams and Williams F1 Team*
McLaren MP4/4	*McLaren International*
Leyton House CG901	*Patrick Morgan*
Jordan 191	*Tom Wheatcroft's Donington Grand Prix Collection*
Williams FW14B	*Jonathan Williams and Williams F1 Team*
Ferrari F1-2000	*Tom Wheatcroft's Donington Grand Prix Collection*
McLaren MP4/23	*McLaren International*

Index

208